D1301671

Portraits of
the Toughest Job in the Army

Portraits of
the Toughest Job in the Army

Voices and Faces of Modern Army Wives

Janelle H. Mock

iUniverse, Inc.
New York Lincoln Shanghai

Portraits of the Toughest Job in the Army
Voices and Faces of Modern Army Wives

iUniverse books may be ordered through booksellers or by contacting:

iUniverse
2021 Pine Lake Road, Suite 100
Lincoln, NE 68512
www.iuniverse.com
1-800-Authors (1-800-288-4677)

ISBN: 978-0-595-42615-7 (pbk)
ISBN: 978-0-595-86978-7 (cloth)
ISBN: 978-0-595-86943-5 (ebk)

Printed in the United States of America

For Steve,
my soldier, my friend,
my husband, my love.
Today I miss you,
as everyday I miss you,
when you are gone.

&

For all the wives, husbands,
and families who serve
and love those who fight
for our country.

A portion of the Author's royalties will go towards the Fisher House, a charity organization that helps support military family members. The Fisher House offers a 'home away from home' for military families, by enabling family members to stay close to a loved one when they are hospitalized for an injury, such as those sustained in war, illness, or disease.

To find out more please visit www.fisherhouse.org

Contents

Preface

Boys Playing in Homecoming Flag

Author's Note

Nothing is more powerful than the truth. Or, at least, that is the hope of the women included within these pages. Their desire is for the truth to be known to everyone about what it means to them to be an Army wife. Beyond the stereotypes and the celebrity military wife, these are the real life words of the girl you once knew in high school who decided to marry an Army boy. There are no big names or big ranks here. The majority of the military is not made up of big names; most soldiers are in the lower ranks of the Army. These women are wives of privates, specialists, sergeants, lieutenants, and captains, all within the lower echelons of the Army. Their husbands do not run the Army; instead, the Army runs them. They live in the Army society, a culture without frills or luxuries, and for a moment they would like to reveal what it means to be a part of the Army. Revealing enough to allow the rest of the country into their world.

Each woman is unique. Their backgrounds vary as vastly as the Army itself. Their education ranges from some high school to Master's degrees. They have a range of socio-economic backgrounds coming from all corners of our country. They are white, black, and brown, but mostly associate themselves with the red, white, and blue. They are daughters, mothers, sisters, and wives. The wives represented in this book have opinions uniquely their own.

Because the Army is such a melting pot, it is not relevant in these stories to list the women with their race, education or their income (rank). Their stories are about their experience as an Army wife, nothing loaded. Rank is rarely discussed in this book because it changes so quickly. By the time the stories come into publication the majority of the soldiers will be different ranks or may no longer be serving at all. Location is relative in the Army. One wife living in Fort Lewis, Washington may be halfway across the globe at the time of publication. Army wives are from nowhere but the Army.

Geographical location, soldier's rank, and position are rarely discussed in these pages for protection. For the safety, security, and privacy of these wives and their families it is important not to tell the world where they are located because many of their husbands are still in the midst of fighting a war. Military families have become victims when too much information is provided or disclosed to the wrong type of individual. Very few first names are used and no last names are included for that same reason. Some of the family members included in the book have been given pseudonyms for their privacy and protection.

There are few defining specifics in this book because each woman, in part, represents much more than herself. A wife you personally know serving in the Army may share aspects of a combination of the stories these wives tell, such as Tammy and Gena or Laura and Alicia. There are hundreds of thousands of Army wives out there, and each is unique. Of course, they all have their own opinions and feelings. By only including the first names in these stories the women become more than just a story on a page, they become a person. The girl you once knew who lived down the street, her name was Amber, married an Army soldier. Do you ever wonder what happened to her? The words on these pages will tell you all the possibilities of what her life has been like over the years; how she has handled having *the toughest job in the Army*.

To organize this book, each woman is represented by her own chapter within one of four sections. Part I includes the stories of wives nearing their husband's retirement from the Army with over twenty years of service. A history of service and many separations, will differ vastly from what they anticipate in the future as they return to the civilian life. Part II includes a large group of women whose futures in the Army are undecided. They range from only a few months of being married in service to many years. For varying reasons, they remain unsure if their husbands will decide to stay in the Army or leave once their obligation has been completed. The tone in Part III changes considerably. These are stories from women whose time in the Army is nearly over. Their husbands' contract have come to an end and they want to get out. These are women who are desperately looking forward to being civilians again and, by publication, most of these women will already be out of the Army. The stories in Part IV come from women who consider themselves to be "lifers." To the best of their best knowledge, their husbands intend to remain in service the full twenty years, if not more. For these women, the future has been decided. Finally, I have included a short narrative about a homecoming ceremony I once attended. While scenes from such occasions are commonly shown on the nightly newscasts across the country, it is a far different experience to be inside one of those giant Army hangars and experience that reunion in person. It is what "Homecoming" is all about.

I am the wife of a Combat Medic working in the Infantry helping to keep the soldiers in his unit healthy and safe. My own unique experience in the Army is included in the Afterward of this book, a miniature autobiography of how I came to be married to a soldier and how it has changed me as a wife.

While you will hear pieces of my own thoughts and experience in the Army, the heart of this book and this story belongs to the wives who have opened their homes and their hearts to the world. They have opinions rarely heard outside of the Army. They have stories, which may change how you feel about Army life and the toll of war.

To supplement the unique context of these stories I have used my skills as photographer and artist to bring a visual aspect to the book. An adjacent photograph or two representing an aspect of the story told supplements each memoir. The photographs contain images of their mementos, their families, and portraits of themselves. They provide a unique glimpse into a world otherwise unknown outside of the tightly knit military community. They capture myriad emotions, burning the stories more deeply into your heart and mind. As the artist, I have chosen specific photographs which I feel best represent the women and their stories to a great extent. My photographic style is unique. Some of the images are extremely sharp, while others convey motion and emotion through time lapse and blurred images. My purpose in including the photographs is to make each woman, each story, that much more tangible, that much more real.

I call these stories miniature memoirs because they are only glimpses into the lives of these women. By keeping the stories short and concise there is no room for exaggeration or fiction. I interviewed these women, entering into their homes and lives, where I collected over eighty hours of oral histories. Their words were recorded and transcribed as they remember their stories to be. When using their recordings I wrote to the best of my narrative ability to supplement and support the stories they told. All of the narrative is non-fictional. I did not perform a background research on the information that they revealed because I felt it was unnecessary in telling their stories. Fact checking isn't important. Emotions are what are important. Their stories are filled with the facts and emotions as they experienced them. This is what our country needs to hear.

Acknowledgments

Nothing can prepare you for writing a book, but there have been plenty of people who have stood by me and helped me along the way. I would like to begin by thanking my husband, Steve. You are the inspiration for my work and all that I do. Thank you for the hours you put in reading, re-reading, and editing this book. I couldn't have done it without you. I love you and miss you so much when you are gone. Thank you for being a wonderful father to our little girl and a supportive husband. We are so proud of you.

I would like to thank the many friends and family members who supported me through the last few years. To my family: Mom, Dad, and Andrew for taking us in when Steve was away and being great grandparents and a fun uncle. Thank you to all the Mocks, Scotts, Howes, and other extended family for being great family and support.

Thank you to the extended family I have made in the Army, especially all the women who opened their hearts and their homes to me so I could write this book. This book is truly for all of you so that you may be recognized for the outstanding job you do everyday as an Army wife. I would like to thank Sandy, Rhonda, Michelle, Laurie, Laura, Jenny, Christy, Alicia, Stacy, Jessica, Katrina, Christy, Gena, Leah, Tammy, Kristina, Libby, Samantha, Nicole, Connie, Tracy, Sheila, Menda, Lisa, Amie, Chrissy, Cherry, Jennifer, Amber, and Carmen. Thank you for your sacrifice. Thank you for your service to this country. Thank you for being you.

There are some people who gave me helpful writing advice that I would like to recognize. Connie Peterson, you are much more than a friendly neighbor, thank you. Sergeant Major Daniel Hendrix, thank you for your touching book about your sacrifice to save an Iraqi boy and your helpful words.

Thank you to all the soldiers and their families. Your hard work and sacrifice is what makes this country so great and so free. I am so grateful and proud to call myself an Army wife and to share that title with so many of you.

Finally, I would like to thank God, who gave me the strength and talent to write this book. Faith is difficult to describe, but it is what I have everyday. I have faith, hope and love in You.

Introduction

Prologue

I began compiling this book long before I ever snapped the first photograph. I took dozens of pictures in my head and listened to countless stories prior to writing a single page. All along, it was a story waiting to be told. The people and the families have so much to tell. In a world full of so much uncertainty and so much change, these families experience extreme change, but do so with pride and strength. They understand that few things in life are certain, except love. The military family is a unique breed of family with many special circumstances of uncertainty. The Army wife deals with that uncertainty in every breath she takes. A spouse in a time of war experiences such a vast array of emotions they almost become numb to feelings altogether. Wives feel everything from joy to fear on a daily basis, yet handle it with a unique strength. Their lives can change in an instant, but still they stand united, proud of the work of their husband. Each wife is different and so is the situation that brought her family into the Army. That is why this book has so many voices. These are the stories behind the story. This is the story of the family support system behind the strongest military system in the modern world. There is a saying among those in the Army, and I am in no way going to claim it as my own. It reflects the true feeling of those who serve their country and the wives who support them every day on their own front lines. The job of an Army wife is "the toughest job in the Army."

For whatever reason, they are what they are, married to the Army. For centuries it has been common to be a military wife. Modern society has allowed the life of an Army wife to become less ordinary and less commonplace. The stories behind the faces in these photographs prove just how unique they actually are as wives. What they endure is also a service to this country and they deserve to be recognized for the strength and support they provide. It takes a certain type of individual to stand by a soldier. According to the Department of Defense, fifty-four percent of the Army is married[1]. The Department of Defense has acknowledged that the divorce rates among married Army soldiers has, "raised a red flag in the armed services. In 2004, nearly 10,477 military couples divorced," up substantially from the reported 7,500 divorces in 2003 and 7,000 in 2002[2]. In this book we find out what type of person it takes to stand by those who fight for our country. You may have strong opinions about war. You most likely have told someone how you feel about the conflicts in Iraq and Afghanistan. Whether or not you agree with what is going on over there, you cannot ignore what is going on over here. These are the real stories and real faces of the soldiers' support system.

I am not the mother of a soldier. I am not an "Army brat." I am a soldier's wife and mother to his child and that is all I have the right to speak about in this story. I realize that there are many other branches of the military. I chose to focus on the Army wife because that is who I am. I also understand that there is a special love a mother or father has for her soldier son or daughter. But I have no experience in that area of the military. I am a wife who is scared. I have a very young daughter who, hopefully, has no idea just how scared I actually am at this moment. My husband is a soldier and he joined the Army during a time of war where it was certain that in the months following his enlistment he would be deployed and be away from us. Now, that time has come. His tour has begun and I am seeking advice and comfort through those who understand and those who know. I am seeking comfort through my camera lens and my keyboard. I would like to bring you along. You may learn a thing or two about this great country and the people who serve it with every step they take. So, please open your eyes and open your ears. These are their portraits …

Part 1

Lifelong Servitude

Wives nearing their husband's retirement with over twenty years in service

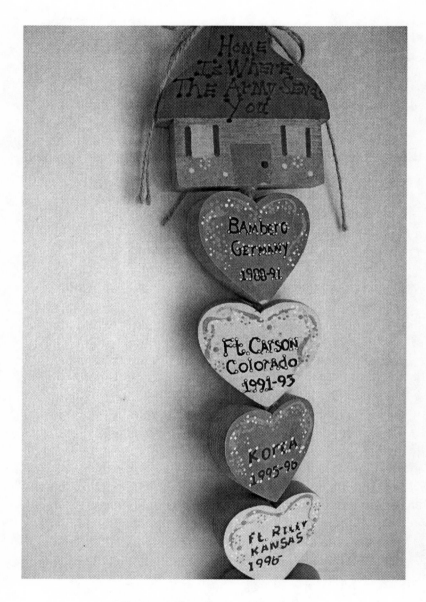

Home is Where the Army Sends You

"I sort of feel like this is what we are here for. This is our goal.
He was brought into this world to do this
and I was brought into this world to,
obviously, support him doing this.
Somebody has to do it."
- Rhonda

Sandy

Hugs from her Boys
Sandy with her three sons

"Him being gone is more the norm than not now.
So, it's harder for them when he comes home
for the first couple of weeks
than it is when he's gone, which is sad.
It's just wrong somehow."
~Sandy

Sandy

"It's been my life and I don't know anything different." These are the words of Sandy, an Army wife who has spent more of her years married to the military than not. "It's really strange for me to go to a civilian place where they don't have any military, and it's hard for me to talk to a civilian because you don't use the same words." She reveals these Army facts of life one windy January afternoon. It is three weeks into the New Year, but it looks more like Christmas in her home. Icicle lights are strung from the rooftops and in her living room their Christmas tree still stands. The extension of the holiday season is purposeful. Her tree stands in waiting for her husband and the father of their three sons to return. It is less than ten days until she expects him to come home from Iraq. She anxiously awaits the confirmation via telephone. She expects there to be a forty-eight hour advance notice to the ceremony, welcoming the soldiers home.

It is just another day in her reality, the Army life. A reality which became her life the moment she fell in love with a soldier while still in high school. She was young when she met and married her husband, Patrick, a man five years her senior. "I was very young. We are one of those rare instances where a teenage marriage actually works. I was fifteen when I married." They wed at the Justice of the Peace only blocks from her school and childhood home. Patrick joined the service right out of school and had already been serving for a couple of years. Her understanding of the military and marriage was limited; she was a new bride with few inhibitions about life.

> "I.was awful. I was a horrible, rebellious person. How I got together with Patrick and not with some other loser was completely beyond me. It was, I believe, God directing my life, far, far before I even thought of acknowledging God at all."

The military felt like home to her, she grew up only miles from one of the larger Army bases in the U.S. The military always had a strong presence in their family. "All five of my brothers joined the military and my sister married into the military. My father was in the military a couple of years before I was born, and we lived near the base almost all our lives, so [marrying a soldier] wasn't an unusual or unknown thing to us. We didn't have any of those prejudices that most people have." Sandy and Patrick have been married over sixteen years now and don't believe in divorce.

Sandy's months as a newlywed were far from typical. While she finished her high school education, Patrick was at war. Maybe she was naive or maybe it was the protection of high school life but, looking back now, she acknowledges how distant the whole idea of her husband at war was to her. "Desert Storm, it didn't seem real. It was so long ago and it was short and just didn't seem real. He left on December 22nd and he came home on May 10th." She remembers because that is his birthday. "So it was a little more than five months but, as far as the actual battle was concerned, it wasn't that long."

She knew little about his time deployed. It was surreal because Patrick kept it that way. He decided to protect his new bride from all the harshness he endured and war he had seen. "I didn't know how serious it was. I didn't know about the things that he had done. I didn't want to know and he wanted to protect me." Many years later Patrick would begin to open up, but only slowly. Bit by bit she has grown to understand more about his time at war and why he shielded her from his reality. "We are talking about a twenty-one year old man and a sixteen year old girl. He's just faced his own mortality and seen things that no man should ever see in his life. He's not going to tell his wife. He's going to protect her as much as he [can]."

Upon his return from the Middle East, Sandy soon became pregnant. When Jonathan was born, Patrick was by her side, fortunate to be with her before they separated again. "From there he was transferred to Germany and this was the beginning of our separation because they didn't have housing for me immediately. I had to wait until they had housing. This was during the Clinton draw downs." That was the summer of 1993, and Sandy fell victim to the tragic floods that covered much of the Midwest. She informed the Red Cross of their situation. "I was staying with my mom at the time, Jonathan was eighteen months old, and our trailer was flooded." The two of them left soon afterwards to meet Patrick in Germany.

"The ironic thing was the day we got to Germany they told him the unit that he had been transferred [to] Fort Lewis, Washington. So, the day that we got there was the day we found out that we were leaving." Even with the discouraging news, Sandy and Patrick were elated to be together again. They soon conceived their second child. "I got pregnant right away, of course." Her due date was the same date the Army gave them to fly back to the states for their next assignment. Sandy was left with the choice to leave Germany before her due date, at the appropriate flying dates before thirty-four weeks of gestation, or give birth in Germany where she would have to wait six weeks until a passport could be made for the baby. "Well, if my husband was going to be in the states I didn't want to be in Germany without him for six weeks. I chose to come back home. So, I flew." Shortly after she had made her decision, the needs of the Army changed again. Patrick was not going back to the states as expected. He would be sent later. Sandy was not discouraged about the potential absence of Patrick at the birth. She thought, "He was there for the first one, he doesn't have to be there for the second one. It was a bonus. So, there I was, eight and a half months pregnant, flying with a two year-old baby and luggage. You know, on a civilian flight out of Frankfurt. Terrified. I was terrified." Sandy feared the flight and being without Patrick again, but she was comforted by the fact that she was going back to Mom and a military hospital in the states.

"They must have really liked him because they allowed him to come home. I was having contractions and my doctor told me that under no circumstances was I allowed to go to the airport to pick him up." When Sandy's contractions unexpectedly stopped, she rushed to the airport without notifying her doctor. She also decided not to inform Patrick about the contractions she was previously experiencing.

> "My contractions [were] five minutes apart and I didn't want to tell him. He's jet lagged, it's four hours after he got off the plane. I thought, 'Oh, okay, I'm going to let him go to sleep.' So, I let him sleep for an hour, but then I couldn't handle it anymore. I woke him up. 'Honey, I can't wait any longer.' 'Can't wait any longer for what?' he said. 'Oh no, we have to go'. We got to the emergency room and our son Michael was born two hours later."

With the arrival of Patrick from Germany and their newborn son, it was a joyful and somewhat chaotic occasion. Sandy understands how fortunate she is to be an Army wife who has had her husband by her side during birth. "I've heard so many stories about women who say, 'My husband was deployed or in the field, or overseas, gone, when I had my children'. My husband was present for all three of my children. Sometimes, just in the nick of time."

The Army shuffled them around the country on different assignments for the next few years. From Germany to Fort Lewis, Washington and from there they went to Fort Leonard Wood, Missouri for drill sergeant training. Patrick's assignment was changed yet again, and he was sent half way around the world to Korea. Sandy and their three boys were left alone living on post. The separation they endured while he was serving in Korea was a critical turning point in their lives, because it was over the course of the months leading up to and proceeding September 11th, 2001.

Sandy held a job at the cafeteria on post. Rumors started at work about an attack, but all of it seemed unreal. She stood in disbelief when the images finally became clear. "When we started hearing the truth about it I was so scared. 'What happens now?' I was thinking, 'My husband's on foreign soil. I don't know what's going on with him. I have no way to contact him. I don't have a telephone number that I can just call.'" Patrick and all the soldiers were informed to contact their spouses immediately. "So, he called me and I was terrified. For the first time in my life I didn't know what was going to happen. The Army had always been this cushy umbrella. You know, guaranteed job, guaranteed paycheck. You always knew what was going to happen. [We] had the comfort of stability, I guess. It was, 'Yeah, your husband's gone sometimes, but you know that he's coming home.'" The world and the Army would never be the same.

September the 11th meant that their lives in the Army would be changed forever. War was imminent. Patrick began to open up to Sandy in ways he had never done before. He began to disclose details about his time in Desert Storm. Things were coming full circle.

> "When they are talking on the news and they are recapping 'This day in history' type of thing, he would get really angry. 'They have no idea what they are talking about. They don't know the circumstances. We tried everything we could.' And when he said, 'We tried everything that we could' it occurred to me, that he's not talking about, 'They did,' he meant, 'We did.'"

After so many years of loving and standing by a man she thought she understood so well she stood face to face with the terrible truth of what he had seen. He was not surprised by the return to the Middle East. "He went to Kuwait in 2002 for the train up and he kept telling me, 'I knew we'd come back, I knew we'd be here again.' I told him that this was a train up and he said, 'A train up for what?' And I said, 'You're training the Kuwaiti soldiers, right?'" Patrick knew that this time was going to be preparation for the impending invasion.

Patrick's unit would not be included with the first wave of soldiers into Iraq during the invasion in March of 2003. Instead, Sandy watched him at home, pacing anxiously, expressing his desire to be there. She saw the fire in his eyes and the passion rushing through his blood, the fire and passion of a true soldier. She is confident that he wouldn't be happy doing anything else with his life.

> "He was a soldier. That was his job. And he didn't finish his job in Desert Storm. He needed to be there. I've had people look at me like, 'Is he just plain nuts? Is he a warmonger? Blood thirsty?' But it's just like anybody else. I mean why do policemen obsess about finding the killer of a baby? It's their job. That's the way they make a difference. It's part of who they are."

His unit was deployed to Iraq shortly after the invasion began, around May. Today, he is again standing on that Fertile Crescent during his third tour. Upon his return home, he has more work to be done in the Army. Patrick will be leaving for an extensive training session before returning home for what could possibly be the longest "R and R" of his life, retirement. When that time comes and he has returned from training, Sandy says that it will have been six and a half years of off and on deployments. They have been together as a family for twenty-two months of those years. It is a lifestyle situation which has changed their children and their marriage forever. Molding a childhood during war has been a difficult task.

> "They don't know him anymore. They don't have anything to talk about. They have new friends that he doesn't know. Things change so much for them that it's awkward. They're not talking to a stranger, but somebody that's not the same person that they knew before. And they've changed so much. I keep him abreast of what they are doing in their lives, but he doesn't know what's going on day to day."

Her older boys have developed their own coping mechanisms that help them through difficult moments unruffled. Her youngest has the most challenges, especially with the many changes the Army life brings. Jonathan, thirteen, tries to fill his father's shoes. "The oldest tries to take control, you know. He's the man, got to be the man. 'Mom, are you sure we can afford that?'" Sandy quickly set him straight after questioning her.

> "But him being gone is more the norm than not now, so it's harder for them when he comes home for the first couple of weeks than it is when he's gone, which is sad. It's just wrong somehow."

Sandy sees the separation as part of her job as his spouse. "The wives have to take a back seat to their husband's job. I don't have to like it, [but] I have to accept it. It's who we are, both of us. This is our life." She has come to accept and learn from this aspect of her life over her sixteen years of marriage to Patrick. She says, "You have to compare priorities. It's all about priorities. It's about growing up and seeing the other person's point of view. The Army doesn't ask you their opinion they give you your opinion. If you don't like it, get out." Sandy feels that many people complain and dislike the Army life because they joined for the wrong reasons and with the wrong expectations. Over the years she has educated herself on how to work with the system. She has seen too many fail because they tried to beat the system. Her opinions regarding the misunderstanding of the Army life extend into the civilian world.

> "I think the problem is that civilians don't understand the military and we fear what we don't know, what we don't understand. I think that they are baffled by the culture. I think they feel sorry for the wives because their husbands are deployed or are going to be deployed and I think that some of them are afraid that could be them. I don't think that [the prejudice] is necessarily against the wives, but against the military in general. As far as most of them are concerned the wives are civilians, it's the husbands that are in the military. They don't understand that it is the whole family."

Sandy believes that civilians have misconceptions about the military because of the way the war is shown in the media. As a wife of a soldier at war, she does not watch the news. It is a tragedy that she does not want to expose herself or her sons to. "I don't watch the news. I get so angry because they don't understand." Patrick has shared his frustration with the portrayal of the war on the news with her. Her feelings grow stronger with each day that he is away.

> "The media has no clue. That's my opinion. You know, they are telling me that my husband is over there for no reason. They are telling me that the sacrifices that we made don't mean squat. That it was useless and wasteful and that the numbers of people that are dying are more important than the numbers we're saving. Who cares about that useless nation anyway?"

Her frustrations stem from the personal pain and anguish that consume her daily life. "I hate war, I do. I don't like for people to die and I don't want my husband to be over there and to be in those conditions." She has become partially numb to his absence. Numb to the danger that entails in his absence. She knows how many good things they are accomplishing while in Iraq. She rattles off a list of projects such as power stations, schools, and sewage treatment facilities. Sandy knows that liberating a country from dictatorship is dangerous, but also very rewarding. Patrick shares those rewards with her, on occasion, over the phone or by e-mail. Regardless of the good he is doing, she wants Patrick home with her and their children. "I would like for the war to be over. I would like for my husband to come home."

After countless months of separation and fear she looks forward to the day that it will all be over. "I just don't ever want to do this again. Ever. We've done our time, it's somebody else's turn." She has maintained her years as an Army wife and mother with grace. Patrick will be eligible for retirement soon and the idea gives her chills. It will be many months until they know when he may be able to retire. That is when he can finally give more attention to his sons, grow in their relationship, and bond with them, as a father should. It will also be a day for her to have more peace in her heart than she has experienced in a long time. She is certain when he reaches retirement that she will still have many of the feelings she has today. She has learned so much, seen so much, and had to be so much.

"Always. I will be an Army wife. I don't think it will ever change."

Big Shoes to Fill

*"The oldest tries to take control,
you know. He's the man, got to be the man.
He'll say,
'Mom, are you sure we can afford that?'"*
~Sandy

Rhonda

Mailbox Full of Letters

"He wrote me every single day
and I wrote him every single day and he was gone four months.
That's 170 days."
– Rhonda

Rhonda

At the end of their driveway stands the only crimson red Oklahoma University mail-box on the block. The blue mini-van parked in front has two magnetic ribbons on the back, one in red, white, and blue, the other simply yellow. Like most yellow ribbons in this part of town, it has the message "Support our troops," but Rhonda also added her husband's name and rank in permanent marker. He is fighting in Iraq.

Rhonda is welcoming and curious. She doesn't believe that her life is anything extraordinary. After eighteen years in the Army, she sits on her living room couch, unsure of what to say. The Army life has been hers since the moment she married her husband, Aaron, nearly eighteen years ago. It has become a part of her. As much as Aaron is a true soldier, she is a true Army wife, able to cope and survive during the most difficult of times in modern history. Her life has been filled with separation, children, and war for those eighteen years.

Their relationship began in high school where they met in their ninth grade biology class. But, it wasn't until she needed a date for the prom that Rhonda and Aaron began dating. A year and a half after they shared that dance, they shared another at their wedding reception. "The Army decided that we were going to get married because he was going to be sent to Germany." He enlisted three months after graduating high school. Through their relationship, Rhonda discovered how he had always wanted to be in the military. It was his dream job. While Aaron was beginning his career overseas, Rhonda was beginning their family back home. Pregnant with their daughter, she stayed in Oklahoma where he missed the birth by just ten hours. "It's really sad when you think about it because he missed my whole pregnancy." Their daughter, Chelsea, was four and a half months old when they were able to join Aaron in Germany.

They would spend three years abroad there; Rhonda experienced the joys of raising a daughter, but the heartache of missing a husband. Conflict began in the Middle East and Aaron's unit was sent to Kuwait. His deployment was sudden and, on Christmas night, he left to Desert Storm. The only tangible way she could reach her husband was with her pen and paper.

"He wrote me every single day and I wrote him every single day and he was gone four months. That's 170 days. You go to the mailbox and everyday you're wanting to hear [from him]. You'd go to the box, nothing. You'd go for three or four or five days in a row [with] nothing. Finally, on the fifteenth day you'd get fifteen letters piled up. It was great to have them. I have them still. I keep all our letters."

To send and receive letters while in Germany, Rhonda would take the bus or ride her bicycle with Chelsea to the Army post. It was one of the many ways she would try to remind her daughter of her father everyday he was at war. She hoped her words and actions would keep her from forgetting. "When they are that age and when they (the soldiers) are gone you have to be constantly talking about them. 'Daddy this and daddy that.'" Desert Storm ended quickly and upon his return to Germany Rhonda's worries came true. Chelsea did not remember who he was. His tour in Desert Storm was only the beginning of many months of separation for their family. Following Germany and Kuwait and training, he went to Korea. Rhonda feels God knew she could handle separation, maybe better than others.

"Someone has to do it. If we didn't have people like us, they (the soldiers) wouldn't have anyone to support them. The people who go over there to fight need support. And I think that some of the best people over there are those who are married, because they know they have support. Everyday they try to maintain their life and stay alive, because they have someone to come back to. I really think anybody can do it, because you have to. That's what you have to do. I sort of feel like this is what we are here for. This is our goal. He was brought into this world to do this, and I was brought to this word to, obviously, support him doing this. Somebody has to do it."

Many years have passed since their time in Germany and his time in Desert Storm and now a new conflict has risen in that same part of the world. Aaron is fighting again in his second tour during Operation Iraqi Freedom. Chelsea is now a teenager and so is her younger brother Dylan. They have grown up knowing what it is like to have their father away for long periods of time. Though Rhonda worried when Chelsea was a little girl if she would forget Aaron, now she finds herself worrying even more. "As they get older it gets harder. When they are little they don't remember it as much. My daughter is really good at keeping it all inside. A 'we can tough it out' attitude.'" It is harder, she says, because they have built a great friendship with their father. When she thinks about the strain the Army life has put on the relationships between Aaron and their two kids, Rhonda knows how much it affects them. It is really the only negative aspect she has experienced in their Army life.

Even in Aaron's absence, Rhonda is comfortable with her life as an Army wife. Not because she can ever get used to him being away, but because she knows what to do when it happens. Over the years she has developed a type of routine to help her cope. She fills her time with projects, whatever she can think of. "I am busy, busy. I put the kids in anything and everything I can." Dylan was recently in a production of the *Wizard of Oz*. "There is never really spare time. I try to do things that I didn't do while he was here, like painting the house. There is never time to think about it, because we are so busy." She has learned that staying active and involved is the key to survival during the hard times.

Rhonda has to maintain her strength through all the difficult moments. For her family, she is the epitome of strength and grace. Recently Aaron underwent back surgery and the painful rehabilitation prevented him from performing his tasks as an Infantry soldier. His unit left for Iraq without him. Those were difficult months in their family because Aaron wanted to be there (Iraq), bored of his stateside tasks. Others outside of the military might see his desire to deploy as strange, but Rhonda assisted him, both physically and emotionally, through those anxious months.

> "I feel like if you had to have anyone over there, he's the one to be over there because he's really prepared. We talk about it. I'm an RN (Registered Nurse). How would I feel if they had me doing clerical work in my job? How would I feel? You go to school to become an RN and you have to do secretary work; you're not going to be fulfilled. You're not happy. He's fulfilled. He feels like he's doing what he's supposed to be doing. He knows there's danger in it and all that. It's hard to take, to hear your husband say, 'I need to get over there (Iraq). I need to get over there.' But I understand where he's coming from."

Rhonda understands his desires. She understands when others in their family do not. Family and friends look at her life, her experiences in the Army, and say, "I don't know how you do it. I could never be that strong." Rhonda is humble about her nearly twenty years of service. "I think I might have different feelings if I knew something different." In a few years Rhonda will get the opportunity to experience the civilian world as a mother, wife and adult. Aaron has a little over two years left until he will be eligible for retirement from the Army at the age of thirty-eight, with many years ahead to pursue different career options. She has trouble thinking that far forward, to retirement, because he is still gone. He is still in danger. When she does look to the future, she imagines herself becoming a nurse practitioner, maybe becoming the breadwinner of the family for a change while Aaron can go to school. They can move. "It's like you've lived so long where you are told to live [that] it would be nice to choose." Choices come few and far between in the Army.

Aaron didn't choose to love the Army, Rhonda knows that it is a part of who he is. Her voice carries the tone of a proud wife. Her house is filled with Army pride and Army memories. Photographs and mementos cover the shelves and the walls. Aaron's new address in Iraq is posted on the refrigerator. Aaron left for Iraq only a few weeks ago. Because of his injury, his doctors were apprehensive to let him go, but following the most recent tests they gave him the go ahead. Less than a week later, he was in Iraq. Rhonda wasn't surprised by how fast they got him out there; he is a leader, in charge of many soldiers. She spoke to him by phone recently, where he sounded tired, but won't say much about how this time was affecting him.

> "He says it is a whole lot different than Desert Storm. It sounds scarier to me. I can't really get it out of him what he is saying, but you can tell this one is a lot tougher. In Desert Storm he was "body-bagging." You think, 'How could it be worse?'"

Michelle

Michelle with John
Deployment Ceremony Summer, 2006

"What do they say? 'If the Army wanted you to have a wife they would have issued you a wife.' Well, my husband lives by that. He loves me and the kids. I have a great marriage. I've been married for almost thirteen years, but he'll tell me 'Mission first.' He says, 'I love you to death, I'll be retired in three years, and then it will be you and the kids first, but until then my life depends on my mission being first.' When he puts it that way, how can you argue with that?"

Michelle

This morning began as many do for Michelle. She saw her husband off to work, her son and daughter off to school, and began her own work from home as a nurse. Her patient is a delicate age, only a few months old. She introduces him as 'Peanut,' her nickname for the very round and grinning infant who is in need of constant medical care. She attends to him briefly with the care and love of a mother, as if he was her own, and then begins to talk. It's as though she's been waiting to tell this story since the moment she met her husband all those years ago when they were both soldiers in the Army. Everything about their family life has revolved around the Army and its decisions. It has been a life filled with more bumps in the road than the average marriage could endure. She has much to tell.

Michelle and her husband Jonathan happened upon their life in the Army in very different ways. While his life's path had always pointed toward a military career, she stumbled into the job. "I grew up in a small town; a very, very small town [in Florida]. Like, one stop sign in the town, kind of small town. My school was kindergarten to twelfth grade. Most of the people I went to school with were teenage mothers ending up on welfare. I couldn't wait to get out." One afternoon she found herself talking to an Army recruiter and within three days she was on the bus leaving for basic training. Her parents were proud of her decision. Her father had served in the Army before and understood her pain and anxieties when she first called home from Basic Training pleading to get out. In a matter of days she was into her new life in the Army with the zeal of a new private, loving every moment of her job.

> "I got stationed at Fort Hood and I went to Somalia; so, I've deployed. It was interesting. I went on 'R and R' and I actually got to get to see parts of Africa. It was a nice deployment. It was actually a UN (United Nations) mission. I volunteered to go. I don't regret any of my military time. If I hadn't gotten pregnant, I would have stayed in. I liked it then."

An unplanned pregnancy shortened her time in service and she made the decision to get out. It was during those moments of first learning about the pregnancy that John became an irreplaceable part of her life. He was also stationed at Fort Hood, Texas. "I didn't want to have a dang thing to do with him when I met him. He was short and I didn't date short men." She was also apprehensive about dating him because she had recently gotten out of a serious relationship. "On John's birthday I found out I was pregnant. I told him, 'I understand if you don't want to hang out with me anymore.' I was all crying and hysterical. 'It's not yours; there is no way it could be yours.'" Instead of the rejection she expected, John went above and beyond to offer her comfort, friendship, and support. He insisted that she, still soaked in tears, get ready to go bowling for his birthday because those were their plans and nothing was about to break them.

They moved in together after Michelle was kicked out of the on post barracks because she was too far along with the pregnancy to live with the other soldiers. In the middle of a health scare with her pregnancy, John told her they were getting married. It was a proposal she barely remembers. "I'm thinking in my mind, 'This man has known me less than three months, I'm pregnant with someone else's child, and both his parents are ministers.' I thought, 'This man is going to hell.'"

They were giddy and nervous, but clearly in love during their simple ceremony at the local Justice of the Peace. Michelle remembers laughing through much of the ceremony. The judge even paused a few times to make sure this wasn't a practical joke of some kind. They celebrated afterwards with beer, a Coke (for her) and a Twinkie wedding cake.

When it was time for their son to be born, Michelle was overjoyed by the response of her new husband towards a son who biologically would never be his.

> "As soon as Dylan was born he was crying. He was bawling. He was like, 'My son, my son.' He couldn't wait to hold him. He wasn't there for the initial getting pregnant but he was there for everything else. I didn't get to hold him for the first two days that he was born because John would not put him down. Then, when we brought him home, I had it so easy because I didn't get up for midnight feedings. I didn't do anything. I only took care of him from the time John went to work to when he came home. I wasn't allowed to touch him."

It was love at first sight. John had a son.

Their time as a family in Texas was short lived. John had high aspirations for his Army career, including entering into Special Forces. They spent the first many months of their marriage in the midst of the most rigorous military training in the world. She knew that John was up to the hard training and she thought that she was too. "He was almost graduated, and while he was gone to Airborne School our house burned down. So I had a six-month-old little boy and our house burned down with everything that we owned. Then he came back and I had a hard time with him being away after that." His long time dream and so much of his hard work were now gone. Michelle felt torn knowing what her husband had just given up for her. "He opted that his family was more important. That says a lot about him."

With Special Forces behind them, they moved on to their next assignment in Fort Riley, Kansas. It would be the base where their second child was born, a little girl. John was placed into an Infantry unit where he stayed for nearly two years until harsh news came to their family. His next assignment, recruiter, came with a strong stigma of breaking the bonds of marriage. Upon receiving word of his orders, the stories passed down from other wives began to run through Michelle's head. "[What] we had heard was, 'Oh my god, your marriage is not going to make it. It was the worst job in the Army.'"

His assignment was in an area outside of Chicago, in a community unlike any-where she had lived before. "[It was] in a rich area so it was really hard to recruit because people had money. They didn't need the military. They had a quota and, even if you make your quota, which is one or two a month, you have to help your buddy make his quota too." She quickly saw how every aspect of his new job was stressful. All of the stories she had heard about the hardships of being a recruiter were coming true.

> "It was long hours. I mean he would go to work at four, five o'clock in the morning and not come home until nine, ten o'clock at night. This was seven days a week; not five, not six. So, we barely ever got to see each other. It was very, very hard on our relationship. I've never seen him so stressed as he was at that time. He even said that he contem-plated killing himself with that job because he was just so stressed and so depressed. He had heartburn and he just hated the job. But John is one of those types of people that, even if he hates the job, he still is going to do his best. He always excels at whatever he does. He may hate it, and it almost cost him his life, but he always excels at it."

He wasn't the only one who was struggling. Michelle never felt so alone in her life. She spent nearly all her time home with the kids for the first part of the assignment where she found herself creating an entirely new problem. She was responsible for all the money since John wasn't available to help. Michelle had learned little about money management throughout her life. It was a childhood raised, as she says, "dirt poor," which gave her no experience to pull from to tackle family expenses with John. On a number of occasions she found John having to bail them out of very bad financial situations. Michelle saw herself as the main character in one of those heartbreaking stories she heard about the life of a recruiter's family. The stories were hers now; the problems were their own. For three years, it became a daily test of their wedding vows. But, where others failed they prevailed. "I know that [during] the time that we were there, there were a good nine to ten divorces. So, that doesn't speak too much to recruiting."

Eventually she began to adjust and even used the time as an opportunity to attend nursing school. It was a short-lived time of stability for Michelle; only one year into her schooling, John was given his next assignment at Fort Stewart, Georgia. This was a major turning point in their relationship and their lives. "As soon as we got to Stewart, he left for Kosovo. Three weeks later, he deploys again. That was the downhill spiral for the next five years." The deployment was as if they were reliving the last three years as a recruiter all over again. John was away and Michelle was left to tackle all the emotional, physical, and financial stress the separation would bring her.

> "I try to not talk bad about the Army. I really try not to because they have been good to us in a lot of ways. But, in the last five years, the Army has changed. I've realized since September 11th that the Army has changed. I mean, they offer counseling and stuff like that, but they needed to do [more] for me; to offer more family time together. Even if it was one day a week where they got off early, but it's 'Mission First.'"

It was the first time he had been deployed since they got married, but distance and separation weren't anything new. He finished his year tour and then attended more schooling before being selected by the Department of the Army to become a drill sergeant. During the many months of training, Michelle stayed in Fort Stewart awaiting his return. Wives and families are not encouraged to move for these types of training.

> "I was at Stewart the whole time, working, and being with the kids. Basically, I had no husband. [It was like] being a single mom, because he's been gone to Kosovo and then to ANCOC (Advanced Noncommissioned Officer Course) and then to Drill Sergeant School. And, when he was in Drill Sergeant School, his unit came down with orders to go to Iraq.

This was when the Iraq war started and we were told that he wasn't going because he had just completed Drill Sergeant School. He had just graduated. So, we had been making arrangements to move, to have packers come, and everything. Then he comes home and he says, 'Unpack.' 'What do you mean unpack?' 'I'm leaving for Iraq in two weeks.' I was mad as fire! I hated the Army at that time. I said, 'I hate the Army. I wish we would have never joined!' He said, 'Well, that is my job.'"

Even with the struggles Michelle had already faced and time she had already spent without her husband, her story continues. For Michelle, there were still many more hardships along her path. Beginning first with John's tour to the war in Iraq.

His unit was the first wave into Iraq. The invasion was everywhere including on television and the Internet. Her own worry was just as prevalent. She did her best to deal with all the anxieties of being an Infantry wife, but she found herself self-medicating through retail therapy. In the rush to deploy, their finances were barely mentioned, and she fell into the patterns of their time in the recruiting assignment. "When he came back, he thought that he had all this money saved up from Iraq. But, he came back and he had nothing." He made his anger known and Michelle feared the worst for their marriage. "I don't blame him. I look back and I was so irresponsible. I was mad and the only way I could make myself feel better was to spend money and shop. I didn't think about anything else at that time."

"I felt that it was justifiable; that, if he divorced me, I deserved it. I will never forget when he left and I said, 'Oh God, when he comes home he's going to say he wants a divorce.' And he came home and he had gone and got a tattoo on his shoulder of my name tattooed on him. He said, 'If this doesn't show you that I am committed, I don't know what else I can do. But, this isn't going to happen again. I'm telling you now, Michelle, if this happens again, I'm gone. Basically, my whole life I've had great credit, I've worked hard, but I can't retire if I have nothing to live on. So, you can work with me and we can retire wealthy, or we'll be apart.'"

His tour was completed. Now, it was time for him to fulfill the duties of his recent schooling, to be a drill sergeant. "Drill sergeant is a week long job; all day long, just like recruiting. We didn't even have time to go back to us being a family.

We just went straight into him being gone all the time." At least, for the moment, he wasn't overseas. He could find a phone more often and call home to say 'hello' and check in with the kids. They used this time to get out of the debt she accumulated while he was deployed. Times were changing. John was making enough money to buy his wife some unexpected, but desired, gifts. He purchased her a house at the post they moved to following his time as a drill sergeant.

Owning her own home is a dream come true. He is retiring soon. They hope, in as little as three years. Michelle sees this being a home where they can continue to watch their children grow up, long after he is out of the Army, and on to his next career. "I still go around and touch the walls like, 'Oh, my house, my house!' [It's] a good feeling because it is the first time I've been able to paint my kids' room whatever I wanted. It's my house." Things were coming together with this new assignment. Michelle was feeling like they were a family again. "And then we got here and we found out that we were going to Iraq. It felt like my whole world was falling down on me again." Her only assurance at this time is that her husband is near to his retirement. "I keep telling myself that he's retiring in three years." It's the hope of the future time together that makes the current time apart almost bearable.

This is where her story has taken her. To a new home that is actually hers, to a new town, and to a new deployment. John is leaving in a matter of days. He is responsible for many soldiers, and therefore, she has taken on the responsibilities of many wives as a part of the Family Readiness Group. The children are not so small anymore. They are young, but aware, of both time and the danger of their father's tour to Iraq. Daddy is leaving his little girl. "For Amanda, it didn't really hit home until they packed their duffle bags last week. She helped him pack. That was hard. She cried the whole time. She was like, 'Dad can't I go with you? I can fit in the duffle bag.' She said, 'Look!' She was trying to squeeze herself into the duffle bag." Both children have each had their moments trying to deal with, and understand, the deployment.

"I've been having a hard time with him going to Iraq. But, then we went to that movie, the 'Twin Towers' one with Nicolas Cage in it, and it put everything into perspective. So, now I don't really have any bad feelings about him going to Iraq, once I saw that. What all those poor people went through and those wives. The only thing I hope is that the car never pulls up to my driveway and says something has happened to my husband. If he doesn't go, then this could happen again, and it could be something with our kids. He said something to me, and I try to keep this in my mind, he said, 'If I deploy now, it may keep Dylan from having to deploy in the future. If I go take care of the problem now, then maybe Dylan or Amanda may not have to go in the future. It may not be a volunteer situation in the future; it may be a draft situation. So, if I can take care of it now, and stop either one of my kids from having to go, then it is worth it to me.'"

~Michelle

Michelle and John Posing for their Son on Deployment Day

Laurie

Laurie Holding Ken on Prize Winning Quilt

Laurie

The indulgent smell of cookies permeates Laurie's kitchen and dining area. She is baking for one of her favorite groups of people, the local college students at her church. Baking is only one of her many hobbies. Displayed all around her home are her creations, sewing and quilting the most prominent. Venturing into her closet reveals years of handmade clothing and detailed creations. Sewing has become more than a hobby or an interest, it is an outlet. With each thread of her needle, she passes through another moment as an Army wife, esteemed and unruffled.

She has healing hands for herself during her many times of need. Healing hands that also make beautiful works of art. Her prized piece is laid out in her guest bedroom. An intricate collage design of yellows and purples make up her winning design, featured in Country Home Magazine during a quilting contest. She won first place, an award which couldn't have been achieved without the help of her husband. While stationed abroad in Korea he sent home the fabrics she used to design and sew her quilt. Fabrics that would have been outside of her price range if she had purchased them in the States. She is humble about her achievement as she opens the window shade to allow more of the autumn light into the small bedroom. She runs her fingers over the colors brightened in the sun, thinking back to the many hours it took, reflecting on the many more hours she has spent as a wife without her husband.

Retirement is a word that rolls easily off the tongue of Laurie, an Army wife of twenty-three years. Her husband, Ken, will be eligible for retirement upon his return from Iraq in less than a year. It will be a turning point in their lives; one Laurie has been looking forward to for many years. She does not have animosity towards the Army. Instead, she is content and committed to the lifestyle as long as Ken is happy with his career. But, there are things that she looks forward to when he is a civilian again.

When Laurie met Ken he was a soldier in the Army Reserves, but he had plans to become a preacher. She met him during college when he was in seminary. He told her, "You're the girl that I want to spend the rest of my life with," in a love letter. It appeared, for the moment, as if she was going to become a preacher's wife. Instead, an entirely different title awaited her. "When we got married he was going to be a preacher but, when he got out of college he couldn't find a job. There were just no jobs available. It was either be in the Army and have benefits or live in poverty." Ken looked at his options for supporting his new wife and enlisted in the Army to become a full time soldier.

Since that moment all those years ago, the Army has taken their family down many paths, many moves, and to many different places. The one that stands out the most in her mind is her time in Germany. During her years in Rosenberg, she found herself volunteering for a number of the Army community organizations. It was the best way for her to meet new people, specifically wives, and develop friendships that would be helpful during Ken's absences.

> "In Germany it was all Army, because that's all you have. I was volunteering with Army Community Service and I was a community-housing mayor. I had to go to town hall meetings once a month. We had to do stuff with the German community too. One thing that I got accomplished while I was there was that I got speed bumps installed on our street, because the Germans would buzz down our street to their apartments on the end."

Dangerous drivers behind her, she spent most of her time in Germany enjoying the culture and raising their young daughter. She collected an array of authentic German objects and mementos which are proudly displayed in her home. Among them a more modest piece of her German past, a piece of furniture. "You don't bring any furniture [overseas], because of the weight restrictions. You use the furniture they supply for you. It's good quality furniture and you can get it for real cheap." The couch that presently has a home in her basement she purchased for three dollars in Germany. It was an offer on furniture she could not refuse.

Scattered among her German collectables is one from a culture from the opposite side of the globe. Laurie would not be able to join Ken on his assignment to Korea. He sent her gifts regularly. Her most treasured piece is a wooden jewelry box that sits in her room. It is one of a number of objects she keeps out to remember his time abroad. To explain the order of his different deployments and tours she points to a handmade string of hearts on the wall. "I used to make and sell these at Fort Lewis." The string of hearts with names of Army installations around the globe has a tiny house at the top. It reads, "Home is Where the Army Sends You." Each base or deployment is listed on a heart. "When I used to sell these I always said that eight should be the maximum number of hearts anyone should have to string. Well, I have ten."

Assignments have come and gone for Ken. His current tour to Iraq is his third, counting his time in Desert Storm. With the time away, both in and out of war, Laurie has spent many special occasions without her husband. Only a few months ago they celebrated their twenty-fifth wedding anniversary, Laurie in her modest home off post and Ken in his camp in Iraq. He sent her flowers he ordered over the Internet. "He was not here this year for our twenty-fifth anniversary this last summer, so he sent me twenty-five red roses." Thinking back to each of their twenty-five anniversaries Laurie believes that they may have been able to celebrate a total of ten together; a shocking number even to a veteran Army wife.

The separations haven't all been dangerous, but they have all been difficult. It has been a marriage, in many ways, of a single woman. Laurie is the one who takes care of the majority of the household details while Ken serves. She is happy to take on the responsibilities, but warns others of the repercussions of not being proactive.

> "You can make yourselves have a tough job by worrying and not learning how to take care of yourself. If you are going to be an Army spouse you have to learn how to keep track of your own checkbook and learn how to do things with a power of attorney. I have bought and sold houses with the power of attorney. That's just a big experience alone, buying and selling a house. It can be pretty intimidating. [You] have to be willing to learn things. If not, it can be pretty tough."

When she speaks about purchasing houses there is a longing in her voice. Owning a home has always been a dream of hers. As an Army wife it is nearly impossible to live in a home for more than a few years. She believes it has been the hardest part about being an Army wife. "Never having your own house. You're in government housing or you're renting. Or you're buying a house, but you can't do that to it because you have to resell it." Laurie looks forward to the day that she can walk into her own home, where she can paint, remodel, and fix it just how she wants it to be. Owning property will feel like a privilege she has finally earned after so many years of service to the Army.

Though she has rarely encountered negative responses from civilians regarding their understanding of the Army life, she does see that there is room for misconceptions. "Ken likes what he does." She has always supported him, but she also has worries of her own. "He may be worrying about life and death situation for hundreds of soldiers, but I am worrying about a life and death situation for me and my daughter." Her most important job through the decades of service has been at home, keeping it a home even when half of that home is away.

She feels that it is important to express that her strength is not all her own. Faith plays a crucial role in her survival as a career Army wife. "I don't know how Army spouses who aren't Christians do it. It's the first thing we look for when we come to a new place. We look for a house next to a church."

Ken has been gone for nearly ten months. He is ranked high enough that he will receive one of the last slots to come home for "R and R," allowing most of his subordinates to visit home before he does. Laurie does not count down the days; she knows too well the unpredictability of his job and the Army. He may or may not even be able to get home for the two weeks they normally provide soldiers. She will know when he calls from the airport, telling her to pick him up. It is one of many lessons she has learned through the years. Lessons in life, love, and faith will help them through the next chapter in their marriage, that of retirement. In ninety short days after his return, he is scheduled to begin his retirement. In this new chapter Laurie hopes there will be a house to call home. She hopes that they will be holding hands on anniversaries. She also hopes that there will be far fewer days quilting alone.

Part 2

Future Unknown

Wives who are unsure of their husband's future in the Army

At the Ball

That Girl

I remember that girl,
we rode the bus,
We'd talk about nothing and
everything at all.

Together, that girl
and I graduated from high school,
And eventually went our
different ways.

I heard that girl
fell in love with a boy,
Who was a soldier,
a fighting man.

I was told that girl
and her soldier married
In a chapel near
his childhood home.

I know that girl
would have been so beautiful,
Dressed in a lovely
long white gown.

I imagine that girl's boy
wore his uniform,
That they made such
a perfect patriotic sight.

I understand that girl's
desire to find love
With a man
who can take care of that girl.

I read how that girl
soon after had children,
Two boys and
one little girl.

I am sure that that girl's
little daughter looks and
Talks just like that girl
I knew long ago.

I wonder if that girl's
fairytale turned to tragedy,
When the soldiers
were sent to war.

I hope that girl
had the same strength
I remember I used to admire
of that girl.

I can't imagine that girl
giving up, but instead
Standing proud
and so strong.

I can see that girl
being wonderful,
A caring and giving,
mother and wife.

I dream of that girl
and I am curious
How will I ever know what
happened to that girl?

Katrina

Kiss-Kiss
Katrina and Daughter Caitlin

Katrina

Bouncing blonde ringlets cover her head and, with her brilliant blue eyes, Caitlin is the envy of many neighbors and acquaintances. At less than two years old she stops grown adults in their tracks. They shower her with praise and even gifts. Her mother is perplexed by the public's reaction to her young daughter. On many occasions, she is speechless in response to passersby's desire to see and touch her little girl. If they happen to be walking down the street carrying a bag of apples, they will give her an apple to share. Whatever they can give her, daughter they do. It is a cultural difference she never anticipated. Oceans away from her home in the states, Caitlin's mother, Katrina, is experiencing daily life as an Army wife in Korea. In this foreign country she gave birth and now raises their first child. All the while the native Koreans stop to witness her bright eyed and blonde haired daughter every step of the way.

Korea came as a surprise to Katrina, but the Army itself was the biggest surprise of all. She met her husband, Rick, while waiting tables at the local Perkins Restaurant during high school. At sixteen, she was charmed by her older manager's genuine chivalry, and marriage came after a couple years of dating. Katrina fell in love with Rick's passion for whatever he was involved in at the time and, only months into their marriage, Rick joined the Army. Surprised as she was at his decision, he was excited for what the future might bring. Only three months after being married, he left for Basic Training. Without her husband, Katrina was devastated. "I was very depressed the whole time he was in Basic [Training], extremely depressed. My sister lived with me and she couldn't stand me. I stayed in the house, I read a lot, and lost twenty pounds. I just couldn't stand to be away from him." It was never what she envisioned for their time as newlyweds. The separation was something she never grew accustomed to during his many months of training.

> "It was the first time I had ever been away from Rick, and it was so long. He only got two phone calls the whole nine weeks of Basic [Training]. So, all we did was write letters to each other. Letters aren't really too much of a form of communication to me, because it's too much after what they are feeling."

Training was an extremely trying time for the young bride. Katrina jumped at the first opportunity to see Rick and live near him. That opportunity arose during his Advanced Individual Training (AIT) at Fort Sam Houston, in downtown San Antonio, Texas. She found an apartment online and, after her arrival, Rick gave her surprising news. "Right when we got there he told me, 'There's another wife that needs a place to stay. So, she's going to move in with you.' I had an efficiency." The two wives shared the only bed in the tiny apartment for months while their husbands trained. "Then on the weekends the guys would come home and you would have no privacy. It was really awkward, but she was really nice."

Katrina was overjoyed to be near her husband again. The emotional roller coaster that began the moment he entered the Army was about to take another plunge. As Rick's graduation date approached, his orders for his next assignment came through. He would be sent to Korea on a two-year tour. "He graduated on a Wednesday and on Thursday he left." Katrina was alone once more. Or, at least that's what they thought. While home in the states on emergency leave they found out she was pregnant with their first child. Rick wasn't going to let anything keep them apart during such an important time. He took Katrina back to Korea, where they found an apartment near base.

"I was unprepared for just how different it was going to be." Language, food, culture, even the Christian religion were all presented in a vastly different light than what Katrina was accustomed to. They lived in a humble apartment since the Army does not provide financial support to family members who come to Korea. Life in Korea was a dramatic change for Katrina. To stay close to family she sent pictures of her growing belly to her six siblings and occasionally called or wrote home. Mostly, she concentrated on finally living with her husband again. Shortly after her arrival, she gave birth. It was a joyous time for a growing family.

Katrina was a mother and a wife in a foreign culture. As she spent more and more time out of the apartment, exploring their surroundings, attention grew towards her daughter. Caitlin was a big hit. Everywhere she would stroller her around the city they would constantly be stopped. "They (Koreans) love babies over there. They're baby people. They'd stop on the streets and give her whatever they could. If they had an apple they would give her an apple. They wanted to give her gifts all the time." Giving gifts to a baby is a sign of good luck in Korea. Katrina was surprised by the generous gestures of so many strangers including money from their landlord to buy diapers. "He would give her sixty dollars every week for diapers." He would hand Katrina the money, and gesture while using simple English that the money was for diapers. Or, sometimes, he would discreetly place the money next to Caitlin, on the swing.

The cultural differences were perplexing to the new mother, though she was grateful for the many gifts her daughter received. Caitlin also received many compliments. On one occasion, while shopping at the Post Exchange, Katrina was approached by a Korean woman who wanted Caitlin to model for a magazine advertisement. "I thought because we were in the PX (Post Exchange) that she was representing the PX." They soon found out that it wasn't for the PX, but a local Korean magazine. "They really love blonde hair and blue eyes because they can't get that themselves. So, when we went there, there were other military wives and all their babies [had] blonde hair and blue eyes."

They keep the published advertisement of their daughter in their box of Korea mementos; a box that contains many photographs of Caitlin's first year of life in her first home. In the box, Katrina also shares the names and pictures of some of the friends she made, mostly Army wives. Surprisingly, they are primarily Filipino instead of Korean. The Korean culture wasn't easy to adjust to during her short time in the country. Some things caught her off guard, like the vastly different attitudes towards Americans. The older generation viewed the U.S. military as helpers and liberators and appreciated her husband and the Army for being in their country. On the other hand, the younger generation would spend their weekends protesting outside the gates of the base. She didn't dwell on the problems or protests of the locals, only on taking care of her family. Eventually, their time was over in Korea, and they returned to the states.

Caitlin was fifteen months old when they left their home in Korea; Katrina had spent nearly two years abroad. The time away from family and friends didn't bother her much. She appreciated the opportunity to be with her husband raising their daughter. "I can say that we have been pretty blessed because considering all the time in the military, so far, we have really only been away from each other for Basic [Training], those nine weeks." That is all about to change. Rick's current unit is scheduled to deploy shortly. It will be a one-year tour.

"It will be depressing for sure. I will try not to be too depressed." She pauses, "I really can't imagine a year. It's a long time." Presently, her plan is to return home. Being closer to family means that Caitlin can get to know her cousins and she can rely on her family for support. While home she hopes to continue with her education, and finish a degree in Secondary Education. "I'd love to teach English. I love diagramming sentences." Her optimism and aspirations to keep her busy are overshadowed by the thought of her husband's impending danger. The separation and the war scare her. "The only thing that we mind about the military is the separation."

Katrina has consistently carried a positive outlook with her during her three years as an Army wife. One primary reason they look to the Army in a positive light are the financial benefits. "Financially, it's really good, especially for new couples. I think it's great financially. We paid off a lot of loans, and [it] allowed us to buy a new car. It has allowed us to save for retirement, and for her school." Not that every moment has been easy. "There are frustrating things. It's frustrating how disorganized it is. I think the wives have a hard time." She empathizes with the handful of wives she has grown close to over the years and the hardships they have endured. She knows that being a stay-at-home mom is a non-stop job, and having a soldier as a husband only adds to the difficulties of daily life.

With all the benefits their time in the Army has provided them, they struggle to decide how long he will stay in the service. Much of the fairy tale has faded away. "We don't want to have to go everywhere they tell us to go our whole lives." Katrina feels this is a pivotal time in his career. His impending deployment and tour abroad will make or break him. She cannot really imagine too far into the future. Instead, she lets her faith guide her. She reflects on how her outlook has changed.

> "It was different [in the beginning]. I didn't know anything about the military. I was kind of excited about it. I always thought it would be a cool thing to be a part of; to be able to go on base, like a fantasy thing. I still think it is, and it's great to support your country."

Caitlin's Big Eyes

Christy

Looking Just like His Daddy

"The kids, they don't ever know what to do.
Their dad's gone or their mom's gone,
they are separated from grandparents.
They don't see a lot of family."
~ Christy

Christy

"She was just eight weeks old when he left. It took us over a year to get pregnant. He was here for the whole pregnancy. That was the toughest part, because he had to see her growing up in pictures. Then he came home during Christmas time, three months after he left. So, then I had nine months to be there without him, and just her. When he left she wasn't doing anything. When they are that small they just lay there. She started to smile the day after he left. When he came home she was taking steps and talking, and she could say 'Daddy.'"

Christy holds her daughter, Kelsey, on her lap in a lawn chair in the autumn breeze. A big hug and a kiss for Mom and she is off to explore the yard filled with fallen leaves. The story she tells about her husband, Shaun, hearing those words in person for the first time, is a treasured moment. Nothing could replace the time he was away from his wife and new daughter, but all the tough times seemed to disappear in those special moments. Shaun joined the Army before he ever had thoughts of a family. Right out of high school he enlisted and has been serving across the country, and the world, for over eight years. Christy came into his life while he was stationed stateside. Christy knew she was marrying a hard working and devoted soldier, and it became more and more apparent as their relationship grew. Shaun was so devoted he used his lunchtime to purchase her engagement ring at the Post Exchange. One morning, Shaun pulled into the driveway after Physical Training, sweaty and tired, and proposed. He pulled the ring right out of his sweaty shoe.

Shaun left his sweaty shoes at home to marry Christy in the local courthouse. Christy knew that planning a big wedding wasn't going to be possible with his schedule. "They are always deployed or they can't get off work. My husband almost didn't get off work for our wedding. No one from the unit got to come. Everyone had to work late." Thrown into the Army life, Christy was initially satisfied with the experience, and they focused on starting a family. She was well aware of the strong possibility of Shaun's unit deploying to Iraq, but starting their family was most important. Expecting difficult times ahead, she developed close relationships with her neighbors and began to get involved in the Army community.

Their first pregnancy came, and so did his orders. Shaun was able to be there with Christy most of her nine months of pregnancy, and was overjoyed to be around for the birth of his baby girl. Once he was gone, Christy would constantly show her daughter pictures of her daddy. At the local mall there is a personalization store, filled with Army paraphernalia. Christy had a necklace made with Shaun's picture engraved on a "dog" tag. While he was away, Christy would point to the photograph hanging from her neck, telling her daughter, "'This is Daddy. This is Daddy.' She called me 'Daddy' for a long time because I kept pointing to myself, to my necklace. So, I was 'Daddy' up until four months ago." Photographs became increasingly important as the deployment continued. Shaun rarely called home.

> "My husband didn't call very often. I would go a month to two months without hearing from him just because he didn't want to wait two hours in line. He doesn't write letters. I got one letter the whole time he was gone. It was hard, because with her first tooth, everybody knew before he did. He was told about her first tooth. The other husbands would find out from their wives. My husband said that it was really hard to call because it made him miss us. I told him that it was harder for me to not hear from him."

Christy thinks back to many moments when she longed for his voice over the phone. She wishes the Army would provide a phone for the soldiers while they are away. "So you could call them, just in case. They don't think about calling." A specific instance during Shaun's deployment would have inspired a barrage of phone calls from Christy to Iraq. While picking up her daughter's first Christmas portraits she received a phone call from her Family Readiness Group. Shaun's wrecker had been involved in an accident.

> "[They] told me that my husband was missing and they didn't know where he was. It turned out that my husband wasn't even in the vehicle; he was in his bed. I was so afraid to have someone come up and knock on my door, but nothing had happened. That was kind of hard. I told my neighbor that if someone comes to my door I moved to Africa or something. I [didn't] want to know. They told me that he was unaccounted for and he was in that vehicle and they couldn't find him. He wasn't there. He was sleeping. And I'm thinking, 'My husband's dead,' and he's safe, sleeping."

Shaken, Christy continued to raise her little girl and continued to fear. Fear was common among many of her friends. In her neighborhood, it appeared as though everyone's husbands were gone at the same time. The emotional toll would create excessive stress among many of her friends and neighbors. "You're in tears because you're stressed out about stuff, and friends are fighting. In the military, when you hang out too much, you end up fighting." The majority of her neighbors had husbands deployed and would rely on one another for companionship. Christy began spending every moment with her friends, shopping, eating, and gossiping. "With my own neighbors, we would end up fighting because we spent too much time together. I mean, we did everything together; we ate meals together. They were all deployed. It's like if one person got a phone call then the other one would get jealous. Rumors were everywhere. It's sad and it's hard." As time passed, it became increasingly difficult for some of her friends. Christy saw wives display many unusual behaviors due to the stress. "I had this one woman who thought that she was going to move her crib up into my house. She lived right downstairs and she was just going to move in. She brought suitcases, like she was going to live at my house." Christy quickly sent her neighbor back downstairs, and tried to help her at a more comfortable distance.

> "For a lot of wives, I found, it's really hard to stay by yourself. They don't like it. I had this one friend who slept on the couch the whole time they were deployed. She wouldn't sleep in her bed at all. I couldn't do that, because I had to have my life go on. If something happened to your husband, are you going to sleep on the couch for the rest of your life? That's not something he would want me to do, sleep on the couch. I have a lot of friends who have a really hard time with the deployment."

Christy was able to maintain an optimistic outlook through the majority of his deployment. She attributes her daughter to keeping her busy being a first time mom and keeping her mind focused on what was important. "Don't dwell on [the fact] that he's gone. Think of the good things that he's doing over there." To help break up the time, she found herself putting together many packages for Shaun. Towards the end of his deployment, she sent him a package full of all his favorites, which totaled more than one hundred pounds. She thought it would be the last package she would be able to send and wanted to be sure it was a good one.

Her positive attitude will be an invaluable asset in the upcoming months. Shaun will soon be leaving for his second deployment to Iraq. In the time since his return, they have had their second child, a son. Now, with two children, Christy knows she will be surrounded by joy and too busy to become unmanageably stressed out. She knows the importance of staying calm. As the adult, she sees how she adapts better to the changes that come with the Army lifestyle. "The kids, they don't ever know what to do. Their dad's gone or their mom's gone. They are separated from grandparents. They don't see a lot of family." Christy sees her children change so much while Shaun is away.

Christy knows change well, now that she has spent a few years as an Army wife. Her life is moderately stable for the moment. However, Shaun's future in the Army is unknown. Although he would like to become a career soldier, serving over twenty years, the Army may tell him 'no.' Shaun has a heavyset build, and constantly finds himself in danger of being forced out of the Army because he cannot make the weight standards, which include body measurements. Christy says, "That's the only thing that I think is wrong. I think if they want to stay in and they can pass the P.T. (Physical Training) test, they can do their job. That is the only thing I don't really like with the military." She sees her husband yo-yo with his weight so often that she knows it is unhealthy. This has caused a lot of stress in their marriage, constantly being unsure of the status of his career. It will be up to the Army, in the end, how long Shaun will be able to serve his country. The Army and a tape measure.

Libby

Cadet Cheerleader
Libby paging through her West Point scrapbook
Pictured in her cheerleading uniform in the center of the page

Libby

"When we got married, we knew that us deploying and being gone was the worst case scenario. I'd be gone, he'd be gone, I'd be gone, and we would have three years apart." The voice of Libby, the wife of a soldier who is a soldier, an uncommon position in the Army. Dual soldiership in Active Duty brings an entirely new array of challenges and rewards to family and marriage. For Libby, she has only barely begun to reap the benefits and drawbacks to being married to another soldier. Less than one year into her marriage, she has every bit of the newlywed blood running through her body. It's that fiery tone in her voice that shows how excited she is about her life. She is almost overwhelmed by the emotional range the she has been through in the last year.

Libby and her husband, Tommy, are both recent graduates from the United States Military Academy at West Point, a post high school experience that equates to four years of basic Army training and college combined. Beyond the blinding white cadet uniforms and rifle firing exercises, it was essentially the typical college romance. During their classes at the academy they met, dated, and eventually got engaged. The first two years of classes at West Point are similar to the average U.S. university. It isn't until the cadets are senior classmen that the experience feels more like service than school.

> "Junior year is when you make your commitment. You can go to West Point for two years and then quit without any obligation at all. The Army is like, 'Okay, thanks for trying.' You basically got two years free of college. I think people should stick it out, which is why they do that. You don't want somebody in the Army for five years who doesn't want to be there. Then, [the] first day of your junior year is when you are committed. You sign your contract and then you are in."

Libby describes that first day of their third year as a pivotal moment. She signed into eight years of service with one swoop of the pen. She knew the moment was coming. Libby had always looked at the Army as a possible career option, but originally planned on being involved in the service through ROTC while attending a state university. With encouragement from a female cadet at West Point she began the application process and soon found her way to New York. For Tommy, West Point was a simpler choice. "He knew that going to West Point [was] what he wanted to do. His dad was in the Army," she says. Her Father-in-law is about to retire from the Army Reserves with over twenty years of service. "He was excited, but it was kind of like, 'This was the next step.' I don't think it was something that he had always dreamed of-being in the Army."

As different as their reasons for joining the Army are, they also found themselves looking at vastly different careers within the Army. Once their junior year was underway, everything felt more serious as the cadets began to look at career options after graduation. Libby's choices were limited because of her gender, which is common in all the military branches. Within the Army women are not able to hold a combat role. "As a woman, I chose MP's (Military Police) because that is really the closest to combat arms of any branch. We can't go Infantry and we can't go Armor. You can go other combat arms, but then you would mostly just go staff." In a staff position a soldier spends most of their hours completing administrative duties. Being behind a desk for long hours was never Libby's intention when joining the Army.

Some of her female peers felt robbed of the true soldier experience because the Army limits the options to women. "To me, it makes sense, just the way that I see it working out. It doesn't bother me personally. I can't go to Ranger School. That's okay. I don't think I would want to go." Tommy is currently away for Ranger School. During a phone call with him yesterday, Libby heard in his voice what a difficult challenge he is undertaking. Ranger training is nothing she will miss. "I definitely felt like my options were open," she says, regarding "hands-on" career options versus support or logistics. "I think it (the Army) has a fit for anyone." Tommy's fit was the Engineers. After weighing his options, he thought, "That would better prepare him if he wanted to be an engineer out of the Army. They give him his professional engineering license just from the time you serve in the Army." The Army would provide a concrete training environment for a career in or out of service.

With their career paths chosen and, most importantly, their marriage coming soon, time at West Point flew by. Tommy was going to wear his uniform in the ceremony. He wanted to look sharp, like a well-decorated soldier, which isn't an easy task right out of cadet school. He already had his Air Assault wings, and wanted more. While Libby spent her last weeks as a single woman touring Italy with her female family members, Tommy went to Airborne School in Fort Benning, Georgia.

The term used in the Army for the formal uniform is "Dress Blues." This uniform is only worn on very special occasions, most recognizably, weddings and funerals. A uniform to celebrate life and to mourn death. The coat jacket of the Dress Blues displays the soldier's rank, unit, and any awards, medals or achievements. In Tommy's case, his newest patch was for his Airborne School Achievement. On their wedding day, in the warm July heat, the two soldiers wed, one in blue and the other in white. While they were celebrating their union, the idea of two soldiers marrying never quite made sense to their family members.

> "I think that people wonder, 'Why would you put yourself in that situation? Why?' I think that for a long time my mom, granted she was happy that I found someone that I love, but she said, 'You know how many challenges [there are] just because of what you do? It would be hard if you just had it yourself, but less than if you both had them. I mean why would you do that?'"

Libby is confident that their love will not be hindered by their career choices. She looks at the many advantages of having a husband who works in a similar environment. "He can support me because he understands. As a platoon leader or as an officer this is what I am dealing with, and he knows it. He knows the dynamics of it. Where as if I had married a civilian, and I was dealing with those challenges, [he wouldn't understand]. It's just so nice for me to have that support, I think." She knows that when they sit down at the dinner table, she will look across to a husband who empathizes with her daily tasks and struggles. Still, she anticipates that there will be many challenges ahead.

> "When we got married we knew [we would deploy], so we are trying to overlap at least a little. We knew going into it that we would have to deal with it, but now its like, 'Here's the reality, here's the orders come down.' And when I told him that I was going [to Iraq] in November, because that was when we were originally supposed to go, that's when it hits you."

Although the specific dates of a deployment are undetermined for Tommy, Libby's unit is scheduled to leave in ten months. In that time she will continue to lead in her new position, as a platoon leader for a group of Military Police soldiers. "I have forty-two reasons to go to work everyday." She is referring to each of the soldiers in her platoon. They are training for a complex mission in Iraq, mostly to train Iraqi police and soldiers. Libby is confident in her abilities to lead and in learning more about the Army. She is not afraid to be in combat though Tommy is extremely wary about his wife's upcoming tour in Iraq. He tells her how nervous he is for her safety and the mission. He said to her, "Send me a letter as soon as you get your mission." He knows that the mission will determine the amount of danger and risk she will endure. "I think that it's, in part, because he has never seen me do any of my job, you know. And I'm good. I'm learning a ton of stuff all the time." Maybe it's the naive heart of a new soldier, but Libby is not afraid to do her job, whether in the safety of her base or while deployed.

Tommy may be leaving for Iraq even sooner. His unit and orders are unknown because he is in Ranger School. Until his completion he will not join his new unit. Libby admires her husband for so many reasons, and is confident in the type of work he does for the Army. She's seen him in action, and while she does not worry about his success in Iraq, it does not stop her from worrying about his safety while training. "I mean, I worry about him now. I don't want him to break any arms, and he's lost fifteen pounds, and he didn't have any [weight] to lose." He began his training two months ago, and still has many weeks to go until graduation.

Completion of the Ranger course means that they will be together again. While she understands the vast difference between the experience of a wife who misses a soldier in training and that of a wife who misses a soldier at war, she is training herself using this trial period to see how she would deal with his absence for a year or more. She has been trying to keep herself busy, remodeling their new rental property and taking on new hobbies, such as learning to cook. "I started to learn Arabic. I know boy, dog, girl. It gives me something to do." Libby acknowledges that most native Arabic speakers would not give her the "time of day" because she is a woman, but she would like to understand what is going on around her while in Iraq.

She hopes that this separation will teach her ways to cope. When deployments do come for the two of them, communication will be difficult. "If we are in Iraq at the same time, I don't think that we would get to talk that much. If anything, it would be through e-mail." With their conflicting schedules, phone calls would be nonexistent.

> "The hardest part [of him being away], I think, and I don't know if other wives who have husbands that are deployed would say the same thing, about being by yourself is at night when you get ready to go to bed. Everything is all quiet, and there is nobody next to you. You think, 'Just go to sleep, and then you will wake up and it will be another day.'"

The seriousness of the jobs they both hold is hitting her harder each day. It controls their future. While friends of hers who are married and not in the military are starting families, Libby hopes to wait for children. She cannot imagine putting a child through the harsh absence of one parent, let alone two, if they deployed at the same time. The reality for them is unique. As soldiers in the Army they cannot look at family, marriage or the future the way an average newlywed couple would. This worries their families. "I think there is a lot of worry. Both my mother and my Mother-in-law are both very concerned, and when I talk to them I get more concerned." They are concerned that baby talk is replaced by talk of bombs. Not that everyone is baby crazed in her family. She feels their parents hearts aching for them, for the separations they will endure, and the trials of war that not just one but two family members will experience.

> "When we got married, [we knew] what it would be like, that there would be huge challenges. But, I don't think that you really understand the reality of what it entails until you are there."

Gena

Spinning Hug
Gena and Daughter

"I was driving down through the town, passed by the church, and there was a funeral going on. Obviously it was an Army funeral going on, because they all had their jackets everywhere, and that's when I broke [down]. That was when it hit me, that this is a big deal. That it's not something that's going to stop. It's not going to slow down. You're going to have to be strong. You're going to have to hang in there because, if you don't, you're going to lose. You can't lose. I think the emotional part of it has been the biggest struggle, but if you have the spiritual part of it, it makes up for it."

~Gena

Gena

She married a private. Gena has had many titles in her life. Daughter, sister, mother. Wife, in-law, friend. Business owner, Medical Assistant, and Registered Nurse. But now, she is faced with one of the most challenging titles, Army wife. A journey that entails many unknowns. A world brand new to her and her children. Their marriage brought them into the military only a few short months ago.

It's lunchtime at Gena's house. Her preschool age daughter, Jaxen, spends her days home with Mom, running errands. They take the other kids to school, and Dad to work, and then they come home. Gena and her family just moved to a new state and city where there is a waiting list to get into the Head-Start program. It's not surprising since there has been an influx of school-aged children in this military based town. Jaxen runs into the kitchen, and brings back a can of fruit, suggesting it would make a wonderful lunch. Gena insists on sandwiches, instead, and returns to the kitchen with her daughter. There is an abundance of room to run in their rental home. Furniture is sparse; the movers lost many of their pieces of furniture. Frustrated and embarrassed, Gena serves her daughter lunch on a picnic blanket laid out on the kitchen floor. She shows off the only existing piece of her dining set, a lonely chair, resting in the corner. Not quite what she envisioned this new chapter in her life to look like; a little too empty for her comfort.

Only a few years ago, Gena was a thriving business owner. "I started my own soap business. Well, it 'shot up.'" She developed a method to make handmade soaps and they were a hit. "I had vendors throughout the state, and I was driving [all over], and it was taking up most of my time. I don't even know how I made it out of college. College, kids, and running around." She was a career mother continuing her education and making ends meet on her own. It had been five years since she was married, and Gena was self-supported, and self-sufficient. "I was at a point in my life where I was content. I was single, I was doing it, I was strong, and I didn't have to worry about financial problems. It was just getting to that point." A point to meet someone new.

While on business, doing comparative shopping at a local Wal-Mart, she bumped into that 'someone new.' She had been there to see how her prices compared to the world's biggest retailer when Dustin approached her. After talking, he got up his nerve and said, "Can I ask a 'soap lady' out on a date?" It was too sweet to resist. They began dating and talk of the future was a prominent subject. Dustin was a welder, but felt unfulfilled and desired a career change. He wanted something that would bring him more opportunity to do things that he dreamed about, such as traveling. He chose the Army. This was familiar territory for Gena.

"I am an Army brat. I grew up with Army throughout the household. My grandfather was CIA. My dad was Army, in Vietnam. We've got a long history, back to the Civil War, where we've got great-great grandparents who fought."

Her family line has served in the military for over a hundred years. Nothing about his desires to be a soldier were new to her. She understood what advantages it could bring to his career and education. She looked to the future as opening many doors and possibilities for the two of them and her children. But she also could not help looking towards the past, what she had heard and seen, as a child.

"At first, I said, 'Why are you going to do it?' I've seen the wounds. I've seen the emotional side of it. I've seen the PTSD, and the bad things. I didn't want to talk him out of it, because if it's something that he really wants to do and he's really compassionate about doing it, you can't stay in their way. They're going to do it whether you like it or not."

At first mention of the Army, she knew he would enlist, and she began preparing for that moment. She prepped in every way that she could and tried to inform herself about the modern Army, how things might have changed since she was an Army brat. She was not his wife when he joined, they did not want to rush things for just the sake of money (married soldiers are paid a small supplement to support their families). They corresponded through his time at Basic Training and Advanced Individual Training (AIT). Following his graduation from AIT, her family threw a wedding together. "We were engaged for a matter of six days and then married." The celebration was short lived. Dustin had received his orders to his next duty station. It was official, they were a couple, they were a family, and now she was officially married into the Army.

They have traveled on an emotional road since their arrival to his new assignment. During this time of war, Gena's eyes look at her world differently than she did only months ago. Not that she ever felt blinded to the reality of war, but now her eyes are more open, they see so much she never expected to see.

> "I went through an emotional time. An emotional time was seeing the faces of soldiers. Not necessarily my husband's, but trying to figure out what my husband was going to go through. I remember being at a stoplight one time, and I saw one of those five tons (military truck) passing by with all the soldiers on it. All had their Kevlar helmets on, and weapons. They were dressed like they were going out. And I saw, the first six faces, which were as if they had no remorse or as if they had no tears or feelings. But then, there was one that just kind of [stood] out. He just stood out from the crowd. His face was still filled with emotion, like boyhood. It was like a child on a truck and he had this gentle smile and was all cheery. He just stuck out. When I saw him I pretty much saw my husband, the naive boyish type, and I felt for him."

Daily life as an Army wife has been a major adjustment for her and her children. Routine has become the key to making it feel more like home, as she thinks it should be. They live off post, nearly forty minutes from where Dustin works every day. Some days she gets everyone into their car in the morning to drop Dustin off halfway to work, where he gets a ride with a fellow soldier. It is an early morning for all of them.

> "We get up usually at 3:30 AM with the kids. Dustin gets up, goes in the bathroom, and flips all the kids' lights on. I linger in bed for a little bit, then I'll go in behind him, and do role call pretty much. 'Ramyle, get your clothes on. Tocia, get your clothes on. Jaxen, get your clothes on.' By that time, I get my clothes on, I'm headed downstairs, and I try to help him to get prepared. He lays some of his stuff out at night. There's some things he forgets, and if don't go behind him and check, he'll forget, and then it's my fault."

The many tiny details have surprised her about this new career for Dustin. Every corner of his uniform has to be freshly pressed and prepped. If he forgets any aspect of his uniform, his sergeants will reprimand him. She attempts to help her somewhat forgetful husband. Since his arrival to his new unit it has been a learning process for the both of them. She always told him how he would be at "the bottom of the totem pole" as a private. It would be a job with very little respect and very little pay for quite some time. With her warnings behind him, she never expected the extremes that her predictions would go. After only a few days with his new unit, he fell seriously ill. "He couldn't make it out of bed without throwing up everywhere." Gena called his sergeant, anyone she could, to try to get some compassion for her husband and allow him to rest. The Army requires soldiers to be diagnosed at an Army medical facility if they are ill or have health issues. That facility was over forty minutes away. Gena couldn't believe her ears. She would have to drive him, vomit and all, to see a healthcare provider who would diagnose him just to simply turn around and go back home.

Gena expected to learn new things about herself as a mother and as a wife when she joined the Army and married Dustin. She knew that it was likely that he would deploy, and she had to be confident in herself that she could keep it together if that did happen. Soon after their arrival to his unit, the 'if' became a 'when.' Only a few months into their marriage, Dustin will leave for a one-year tour of duty.

> "If this is what he wants to do then I am behind him one hundred percent. Two hundred percent, if that's what it takes. But, a lot of it concerns me. I am worried about the death toll there. I am worried about my husband walking into nothing but gunfire, because that's more or less what it is. Roadside bombs scare me. I don't feel like he has enough training. He, himself, and his upbringing is probably the training that he needs. Not that the Army hasn't given him good training, so far."

Dustin expresses to his wife his confidence in himself and in his fellow soldiers. Each day he comes home exhausted, overrun, and challenged by what his job requires. It is a challenge he enjoys and takes pride in. A pride which Gena knows will be helpful for them both in the upcoming months. It is a scary time and, understandably, Gena is not as confident as her husband. "He wants to serve his country and he wants to be there for these others who can't. I think that's commendable, but at the same time, I'm watching my husband walk into the line of fire." Dustin will deploy with an Infantry unit, the ground soldiers who she sees as being in the most danger. However, he is not an Infantry soldier. While in Iraq, he will be a driver. While his hands will be on the wheel and on the gears, he will have no hands to fire his gun or to protect himself. Truck driving is viewed as a dangerous job in the Army. Gena insists that this position, with little protection, gives Dustin the ultimate test of faith.

Faith has been a marked subject. Dustin has expressed his confusion on the biblical definitions of killing, sin, and war. His upbringing and faith have always told him that killing was a sin. Gena fears that her husband's faith may prevent him from coming home alive, something she believes his religious upbringing never intended to. "I had to sit him down and say, 'No sin is greater than any other, and what you've been called to do is what you've signed up to do. And I'm sure God's going to understand if you're defending yourself, your country, and you're saving lives.'" She can only hope that his training and adrenaline will help him through the dangerous moments and overcome the questions he has about sin and war.

> "My dad is probably the reason why Dustin was pulled out of the whole, 'I don't think I can kill somebody' type situation. My dad said, 'You make sure *that* guy dies for his country and you come home safe. You make sure *that* guy dies for his country and you pull your man out of there.' You know, that's what a war is. You're going to make sure you are going to protect yourself and the other people [around you] and make sure you come home. My dad is probably more emotional about it. He's been in combat. He's pulled men out. And, he's laid in a field for three days (injured). He's one hundred percent disabled (from Vietnam)."

Gena's experience growing up as an Army brat will be an asset to the many challenges ahead of her. She saw in her childhood the emotional and physical burdens of war. Faced with her father's troubles preceding his duty in Vietnam, they have become powerful memories. He stayed in the Army for many years, as a Reservist, until his body finally gave out on him from the side affects of Agent Orange and diabetes.

> "We'd tease him about being shot in the butt. He's got a Purple Heart for it. He actually got shot and pulled somebody out at the same time. Then he was shot again, in the head, and laid in a field for three days, and then someone pulled him out. He did come home with a Bronze Star, and other types of things, and was very commendable. But, I saw the things it caused in our household."

Dustin is scheduled to leave in a number of weeks. Gena does not dare count the days. Instead of focusing on her fears, she busies herself. "When you are a married, a single mom, you've got a lot of things to do." There is a list in her mind of many things she can accomplish in the upcoming months. She looks around her and points out aspects of their rental property they hope to renovate. Her eldest son, Trey, who has been living with his grandmother in order to complete his sports season, will be joining them shortly. Gena, who is already a Registered Nurse, would like to pursue her education further. She thinks about a career in teaching. "What I want to do is be a science teacher. Be a professor at a college, teach sciences, and eventually move into teaching nursing." Her four children and her career aspirations will fill every moment Dustin is away, but when you live in a military town, there are constant reminders. She will feel his absence and miss her husband.

Leah

Leah Cuddling Her Poodle

Leah

Leah is a proud Mama. Her little girl, Paige, snuggles in her lap. With her strawberry blonde curls consuming her, she is her mother's favorite girl. "She was Valedictorian of her training class and got a gift certificate. We are going to go to the pet store today to get her a special toy." Paige, her miniature poodle, is her little one while she and her husband wait to have children. Her husband, Scott, has his own little girl. A collie mix named Naomi. They are a young couple with a bright future ahead of them. Hopefully, children are in that future but, for the time being, they are planning to wait. Wait until Scott doesn't run the risk of being away on tour, and wait so that Leah can pursue her Master's degree from a local university. Motherhood is something she looks forward to when the time is right. When Scott has left the Army.

On this afternoon Leah wrestles and plays with her puppy on the couch. Their two dogs will make wonderful companions in the coming months. Scott is on his way back to Iraq. The adjustment to war is not a new challenge for these newlyweds. Shortly after they were engaged, he was sent on his first tour of duty. "He proposed to me in January and we were still separated [because of school]. Then a week after he proposed he found out that they were going to Iraq. This was January of 2003, right after it (the war) started. They had just started to get things set up over there." Leah and Scott met in college in the second week of her freshman year. While Leah was thriving in the university experience, he was struggling, both with the cost of tuition and the rigor of his classes. Seven months into their relationship he left for boot camp to join the Army Reserves and receive tuition assistance through the G.I. Bill.

The new Reservist would be one of the first soldiers to join the invading forces in Iraq. He left shortly after his individual training, with little information to relay to his fiancé. It was a difficult goodbye. Leah was living a day's drive from where his Reserve unit was located and, with each visit, they knew it could be their last opportunity to hold one another for many months. She kissed him, held him, and cried with him three times before it was their final goodbye.

He was sent to the northern regions of Iraq, where soldiers had only begun set- ting up camp. Communication with the outside would have been nearly impos- sible, but Scott brought his cell phone to war. With a dollar a minute plan he called Leah from Iraq. They had many conversations, they stayed close, and she knew that he was safe. Those talks on the phone may have been the only way she made it through the deployment.

> "He called almost everyday. That really helped, but I had a really bad attitude almost the whole time. I hated the Army. I was like, 'I hate the military, and I hate what they'd done.' I wrote letters to Senators about how he needed to come home. It was just at that point we (the United States) had chosen to do this (the war). I mean I wasn't married to him yet and I never thought about not being with him. I was mad at him for leaving me for two years. I am determined this time that I am not going to have that attitude."

Scott was in Iraq for nearly fifteen months of duty. Leah collectively counts the time spent training and deployed, and considers herself to have been separated from her fiancé for over two straight years. It was two years of being alone, in part, because she felt alienated from her classmates and professors. "The people there (her university), because they didn't have much military, they didn't really know, and they didn't really care. It hurt my feelings that people there didn't under- stand." Her main coping mechanism was Scott himself, writing to him and talk- ing to him. Leah explains that it wasn't fear that consumed her. Instead, it was the pain of simply being without the one she loved. His position in the Army is one of the least dangerous.

> "It was more difficult day to day with boot camp than with Iraq because I had never been afraid of him dying in Iraq. I know I could die easier in a car wreck, and I know that God has a time plan for when we're going to die anyway. So, I can't change it. I can pray for his safety and every- thing, but it's not something that I worry about, him dying. I mean he's a Chaplain's Assistant, so he's not really on the front line, anyway. If he was on the front line than I might be a little more concerned."

Leah believes that the position of the Chaplain's Assistant is a good fit for her husband. He aspires to become a pastor in the civilian world after his time of service. Even with the difficulties he has endured as a soldier she has been happy with this path. "I think I actually like this route that God has taken us on. Even though it's been really hard, in retrospect, I like it because it has gotten us ready. I have finally let go of myself enough to be a pastor's wife. It's a very selfless job. I wasn't ready to be so selfless."

Following his return from war they were married. He arrived back in the states just in time to see her graduate and took time off to take a trip to Disney World for their honeymoon. With war and college behind them, they looked towards the future. Soon they considered joining the Army full time. It was a decision triggered with emotions brought on by an incident at a hospital. A soldier from his unit was facing tragedy; his young son was in emergency care after being run over by a lawn mower. The unit's Chaplain was unavailable and, as the Assistant, Scott was sent to help the soldier and his family.

> "We went to the hospital to visit them and he actually recovered. He is doing really well. He was only four [years old], so a lot of the scarring will heal and he will grow. Just to talk to them and be there to pray for them, it was awesome. We were helping people. It was like we were pastor and pastor's wife, which is our ultimate goal. He was like, 'I want to do this full time.' We wanted to go Army full time so he could do that full time, but it has been a lot different than he thought it would be."

Their decision was immediate. Leah left her job and Scott became Active Duty. Boxes were packed and the movers were shortly on their way. Active duty would not be a new world for Leah. She had experienced it as a child in a different branch when her father served. "He's been in since I was born." Her father, who is currently an Air Force Colonel, has those above him wanting to soon make him a General. "The Air Force is a lot different than the Army, or at least that is what it seems like. With [my father's] job he didn't have to move around a lot. He didn't leave for more than a month or forty days at a time." Scott's father had also served in the Air Force, and he initially hoped to follow in his footsteps. When the Air Force recruiter's door was closed the day he went to enlist, he walked over to the Army's office, and joined with them instead. Much more thought and planning went into their decision to join Active Duty. The excited couple was ready for his new assignment, but never imagined the difficult times ahead.

> "He's had a rough time transitioning from Reserves to Active Duty. It's very different. He kind of got picked on for a little bit, because of his transition. He wasn't in good physical shape, because they (the Reserves) didn't have to do it (physical training) everyday. He doesn't like to work out. But, Chaplain's Assistant seems to be a difficult position, in gen-

eral. No one knows what they do, but the Chaplain's Assistant. People have a hard item defining what they are supposed to do. He thought he was going to love it. He doesn't. I mean he likes it, but because he doesn't love it; it gives him a chance to refocus on his schooling."

She understands what an important time this is for his career, and hopes that his service will become a great resume builder when he decides to re-enter the civilian world. "That means when he goes into his interviews to be a pastor, he won't just be some kid out of college. He will have been through war twice. He has a family. He has graduated." Leah understands the resumé for a pastor includes his family too. She has seen the many positives for their relationship, the growth that the Army has provided them, as an asset to his future career aspirations. "I mean when we got married we were kids, we were eighteen years old. He was very immature, so was I. The Army has matured him a lot quicker, and he continues to mature."

The continual growth and maturity for Leah has been a challenging topic. On occasion, she fights and resists the Army with all of her heart. The lessons she learned during her experience of his last deployment will be irreplaceable in the upcoming months when he leaves with his new unit for a year tour. It hasn't been easy for her to face the future, to imagine his absence again.

"When I first found out [they were leaving for Iraq] I couldn't get it out of my head. I basically started detaching myself from him; like, to let him go. Then I kind of had to smack myself in the face, because he wasn't going to be leaving for six months. That's half of a deployment. 'You need to get it together and not do that.' So, I really put it out of my head, and I think it still is kind of out of my head right now. I think it kind of hit me yesterday at the Commissary, and last night at bible study, when we were praying for him. At the Commissary, when I saw the guys in their DCU's (Desert Camouflage Uniform), I kind of got the old pain of him being gone."

Leah admits to her depression, and is an advocate for herself. She plans to seek counseling while he is away. "I should have last time (while he was deployed)." Her attitude has matured. She no longer hates the Army or blames the Army for Scott being sent to war.

Today, she is focusing her time on preparing and planning for how she will cope. She purposefully rejects the naive and negative thoughts that once filled her. Now is the time to be a family and concentrate on togetherness, instead of the separation ahead. The Army life has been a struggle for her. She describes the sometimes agonizing moments of being married to the military. "The pulling around of your heart, the tugging of the hope, and the shattering. And the uncertainty, and how slow they are at figuring things out. It's just a mess. I've learned not to expect anything until they've got their orders, and to prepare yourself for the worst."

Tammy

Children's Ornament Front

Children's Ornament Back

Tammy

*Tammy's family Christmas tree is covered in holiday fare and topped with a bow. Lighted and decorated with a variety of ornaments, it is the centerpiece of her living room in the weeks leading up to Christmas. Many of the ornaments belong to her children, reflecting their current hobbies and interests, like a glass soccer ball. Some of the ornaments are even handmade and colored by their hands with love. A few made by her children spent their first Christmas hanging up in Iraq during Chris' deployment, nearly two years ago. Special notes are on the back of each ornament, wishing Daddy a Merry Christmas, telling him how much they miss him. Another ornament catches the eye. Shiny metal, it is a "dog tag," hanging in the branches. One of its sides makes a statement all her children feel. "*PROUD TO BE A MILITARY KID.*"*

This Christmas will have added meaning because the family is together as a whole. For over six months Tammy's husband Chris has been told he would deploy to Iraq between Thanksgiving and Christmas. Eventually, rumors began, even on the national news that Chris's unit would not be going to Iraq, yet. While enjoying Thanksgiving dinner, Tammy received a call from her mother. "My mom calls to tell me that [Tammy's uncle] called to inform her that they just had a thing about our soldiers not being deployed until January or until the later part of next year. It was on CNN." Tammy was dumbfounded. "They don't tell us [anything]. Our guys were the last ones to find out." In that quick moment it went from a casual turkey dinner, to moments of many thanks and relief.

Their family had much to be thankful for on that Thanksgiving evening, but it wasn't quite that simple. Tammy has grown to understand what unknowns come with the Army life. During the last deployment they were given three weeks notice. This deployment they were given six months notice then it was postponed at the last moment. Her knowledge of the military has grown exponentially in the years since her husband joined. She feels her perspective in the Army is unique because, when her husband joined, they had already been married ten years.

"I've lived on both sides. I've lived twenty-nine years on the civilian side. While most women have lived most their lives on the military side, and really never focused on the civilian side, never had to deal with [it], I have been through it all."

Prior to enlisting, Chris had a stable and successful job for a door manufacturer, but the terrorist attacks changed things for them. He joined three years ago, following 9-11. The transition into the Army life came with its ups and downs. Tammy had to make adjustments to her own career as a Kraft Foods representative, and the children had to adjust too. The obvious change was their father's absence. Whether because of training or deployments, it was a dramatic change, after spending so many years in the civilian world. Tammy believes that they began to get used to it, but that didn't mean it was easy.

> "It was a lot harder. They basically went from dad raising them to mom raising them. And it was just a lot harder on me, the stress of not having him there. We've dealt with everything. We'd talk to him as much as we could on the phone, and letters, and e-mail everyday. [There were] a lot of e-mails and care packages."

Thinking about the care packages she would send Chris while deployed brings back joyful memories. "Kool Aid. He wanted plenty of Kool Aid. During the holidays it was candy corn, as much as I could get, and jelly beans. [Those are] his favorite two things. Luckily he didn't get a cavity, but he was constantly [wanting] sweets." Tammy would consistently supply her husband's sweet tooth, spending upwards of seventy-five dollars on each package she sent. Their children loved to help, and filled the boxes with cards, stuffed animals and Christmas ornaments. Chris was overwhelmed by the amount of letters he received while in Iraq. "He got cards from people that he had never heard of before, but they were all from the different churches back home, because his dad's a Doctor of Preaching. Everyone [he has known], from the time he was a baby until now, was sending him cards and cookies and everything."

Chris' deployment was a time for Tammy to spend focused on her children and on herself. She developed many rich friendships, which introduced her to a different side of the Army. Her friends revealed the harsh effect of war on marriages. "I used to hang out with a bunch of my friends, but they're mostly gone now. Their husbands went to Iraq, and they filed for divorce, so they are all gone." She thinks back to an article she once read which supported her observations. "They rated this base, one time before, when our guys were gone to Iraq. This [base] was the number one divorce rate for United States Army bases. It was really high. I can say of the majority of my friends I've known, ever since I moved here, [that] more than half have gotten divorced. I guess it's the stress of it." She empathizes, but manages her stress all the same. "You do get a lot of stress while they are gone, but my stress started the day he left for boot camp."

Communication with Chris helped her remember what was truly important. Tammy kept her cell phone by her side at all times, missing only one phone call the entire year. She would e-mail and text message Chris whenever they had the opportunity, even if it was while driving in her car. "A lot of it [was] done on my cell phone. I'd be driving from here to Tennessee, my cruise control set on ninety, and I'm sitting there typing to him, going down the highway." She doesn't recommend it to anyone, noting that it was much safer when she would pull over to a gas station.

Many months have passed since Chris' return home. Tammy has grown in her involvement and in her understanding of Army life. She has become a Point of Contact for her husband's platoon and provides a flow of information for wives. During the last few weeks when their husbands were finding out the deployment was delayed, Tammy had many rumors come her way. "The rumors that are going around. Oh my God, I have heard every little story that could be imaginable." She smiles. "The best way to tell you that they are leaving is when your husband comes in, and packs his other bag, and says, 'Honey I'm leaving in two weeks.' That's the best rumor that you could ever hear."

Time has given Tammy the opportunity to see the many advantages of their decision to join the Army. Dramatic events have happened back home, factories closing down left and right, and pink slips are abundant. She sees job security as a growing advantage in the military, because of what is happening to many people she knows back in their small hometown in Tennessee. She believes that there is a lot of confusion about the Army. For her and her family it comes down to the basics. "The difference between civilian life and military life is, [in the] military we get free health [insurance], and we've got security. We know whether or not our husbands or wives are going to lose their job overnight." Her friends have been confused by their joining the Army and ask her why.

> "We try to tell a lot of people this. Our friends that are civilians, they don't understand. They'll be like, 'Well, you don't make that much in the military.' But, if you turn around and look at it, we get free housing, free utility bills, and free insurance, and one of the best educations in the world. That should sum it up, you know. That is the difference between civilian life and here."

Along with the security she feels, the educational opportunities are impressive, such as the scholarships and grants offered to both soldiers and their spouses. Tammy is studying for her Associate's Degree on post. "It's easier on me and on us [as] military, rather than [as] civilian. I just think that the military does so much for you." Because Tammy has lived this somewhat split life she has the unique perspective to see both sides clearly. Right now it is clear to her and Chris that they are staying in the Army. He plans on reenlisting soon. Filled with excitement she says, "We want Hawaii. Yes, we check the temperatures like every other day. This morning it's five below zero wind chill here and only eighty degrees there."

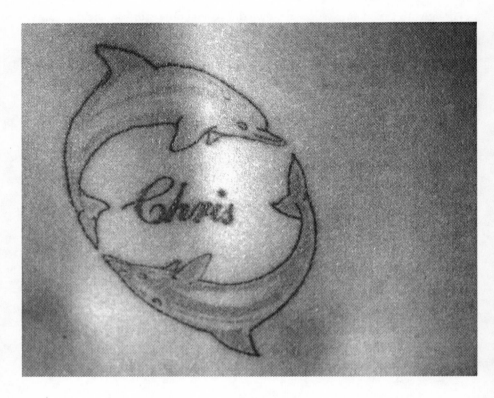

Chris Tattoo
"Chris" is one of two tattoo's Tammy has of her husband's name

"I used to hang out with a bunch of my friends,
but they're mostly gone now. Their husbands went to Iraq,
and they filed for divorce, so they are all gone."
– Tammy

Kristina

Kristina and her "Babies"

Kristina

Few Army wives look at a uniform the way she does. The Army's Desert Camouflage Uniform, called DCU's, symbolizes much more than combat and war to this wife. She sees more in the tan colored uniform covering her tall husband than mere recognition of his service in Iraq. She has seen it in her own reflection. Once a soldier, she too wore DCU's and served in Iraq. As a soldier, she marched and fought. Now, as a soldier's wife, she looks at the Army through the tan colored glasses of a woman who has seen combat, and it alters her perspective on marriage in the military. Kristina is a wife who is also a veteran.

There is snow outside, and although the sun is shining high in the sky, the air is crisp, and some of the glistening snow has begun to melt. Kristina and her husband, Matthew, own a home in a small town adjacent to post. A statue of a soldier holding the U.S. flag stands in salute on their front lawn, marking the house. A soldier lives here. Inside, Kristina comforts her Husky who is recovering from surgery and watches as her new kitten bounces around the living room attacking Christmas presents at will, overjoyed with each successful attack.

Today is another day filled with unknowns. Kristina, who has been recently laid off, is hoping that the next call to her phone will be her boss asking her to come back. Her job for the past few months has been with a company contracting through the military. It required that she work on post with many soldiers on a daily basis. She enjoyed the job for many reasons. Primarily, it was the closest thing to being a soldier since her discharge from the Army. Just working with soldiers and being on post helps her overcome many of the challenges she has faced. It was never her plan to get out of the Army. "It's hard because I really wanted to be in for my twenty years, but it just didn't work out that way." The position she has held for the past few months as a contractor working on post has helped her mentally and emotionally. Crossing through the post gates each day, interacting with soldiers, handling guns, it all feels like the life that she once had as a soldier. It feels like home.

She did not begin her journey with the military by choice. Her father served in the Marine Corps for over twenty years, a distinct lifestyle which instilled values she hoped to carry into her own career. He had set an example of discipline and respect, which she hoped to find in her own twenty years as a soldier. Kristina first became a soldier through the JROTC program where she spent four years learning the ins and outs of the Army. Shortly after enlisting in the Active Army and arriving at her new unit, orders came for a tour in Iraq. Training became more rigorous as they prepared for the mission. To escape the Army world she found herself off post trying to meet new people, eventually meeting another soldier, and her future husband, Matthew.

Though the couple hit it off right away, they believed the romance would be short lived. "I got orders to go to Iraq and he was supposed to go to Warrant Officer School, so we pretty much said goodbye. I went to Iraq and then guys [in his unit] went to Iraq." Kristina was confident that she would never see him again. She focused on the mission, familiarizing herself with the culture, the people, and the task at hand. It was a very different war than what she believes it looks like today.

> "When we got over there, we were the first push, so it really wasn't that bad. People really could walk around without their gear. You weren't supposed to, but they could and you'd be safe. Now, it's way worse than what it was."

The impression of war still consumes her. The reality she took back with her, the smell, the taste, the sights, and sounds, are what set her apart from other wives in the Army. She became a wife shortly after her return from war. Matthew had not gone to Warrant Officer School and instead had spent nearly the same months she did in Iraq, on his own mission. When word arrived that his unit was scheduled home Kristina decided to surprise him. "I met him at the hangar, and he said, 'Wow, I wasn't expecting to see you.'" It was a joyful homecoming and their relationship quickly became serious. A few months after his return they married at the local courthouse, only miles from the post where they both worked. The future appeared bright and clear for the dual soldier couple. It was a wonderful time in their lives.

Then, Kristina's body began to change in ways she had never felt before. They became increasingly worried about her health. "I got 'med boarded' because I got asthma over in Iraq, or else I'd still be in. I'd be over in Iraq right now." It is a condition experienced by many of her fellow soldiers. The diagnosis has been a major adjustment in her life. She lost her dream of becoming a career soldier, and it effects every moment of her daily life.

> "I can't really exercise as much as I used to. It really sucks. I tried last month. I took the dog [out]. I took her to the end of the street and back, and I thought I was going to die. A lot of people got it over there."

Her drive to be a soldier made her a unique woman. Now, the fact that she is an Iraqi war veteran makes her a unique Army wife. Kristina's heart is in a different place than most of the wives she shares the room with at her FRG meetings. During the most recent meeting regarding the impending deployment in a few months the other wives' eyes are filled with worry. Instead, her eyes have confidence and understanding. Matthew will be on his second tour. Although she knows the risk of war has changed since his last deployment, she fears little. At those meetings she converses with Matthew's commanding officer's wife. They have the one thing in common which sets them apart from all other wives in the room. They talk and understand one another's perspective because they are both veterans. They know and complain about the structure, the rules, the regulations, and the politics of daily Army life.

Kristina has difficulty empathizing with many of the Army wives she meets. She admits that, "Most of my friends are in Iraq. They are Active Duty. I don't really get along well with females." In the Army, the words 'men' and 'women' are rarely used; it is all 'male' or 'female.' As a female soldier, and now a wife, she has seen what war can do to relationships, from both sides. The most heartbreaking are moments when her soldier friends return from war to find someone else sharing a bed with their wife. Now, as a woman married to a soldier who is about to leave, she has even less compassion and understanding for those particular women. "I don't know why wives can't stay faithful to their husbands while they are gone. I still haven't figured that one out. I know that you get lonely, but come on now. I see it a lot."

Looking towards Matthew's future deployment she anticipates that she will do well. Eventually work will keep her busy, and she plans to begin pursuing higher education. Her childhood gives her confidence. She can draw on her many years as a Marine Corps brat, when her father would be gone nearly every six months. "Maybe that's why I can deal with it better than most people. Because I'm used to the people close to me being gone." Obviously, her emotions will be different as a wife, instead of a daughter, of a soldier who is away.

"I am, but I'm not [worried] because they've been there, and I know how it is, and the Iraqi's want us there. It's the guys from other countries coming over bombing us really, and the few that are on Saddam's side. But the Iraqi's, for the most part, they are glad we are there and they want us there. They want the help and they tell you that all the time. People over here just don't understand."

Kristina mentions a series of protests at soldiers' funerals specifically, that she has read about, and seen in the news. For many reasons it infuriates her. As a veteran, and now as a wife, every incident where she feels that soldiers are disrespected tears her apart. "I thought that was ridiculous. I can't believe that." Kristina can only imagine how upsetting it must have been for those soldier's family members.

"The guy is dead and they are protesting at his funeral. Come on now, have some respect for the dead and the soldiers. They don't understand. They just think that we are over there for no reason. And, most of the younger soldiers that are over there now, enlisted or re-enlisted after 9-11. So, they knew, 'Hey, I'm going to Iraq. I'm going to Afghanistan.' So, we raised our right hand and we knew what we were getting into when we did it, and people just don't understand it."

Where she is going this afternoon people do understand. Matthew just arrived home early from work. He will drive his wife nearly two hours to the nearest VA hospital. On a snowy day like today it may take them twice as long. During her appointment Kristina will take a survey which will determine what type of treatment she receives for her many symptoms following her deployment. She expects that it will be a long road ahead to feel even half as strong and healthy as she once did. With Matthew by her side, she knows she can handle all the difficulties that lay ahead.

Iraqi Freedom Boonie Hat

*"I am, but I'm not [worried] because they've been there,
and I know how it is, and the Iraqi's want us there."*
-Kristina

Stacy

Hugs Goodbye for Change of Command

Stacy

In the chapel kitchen, Stacy rinses dishes and fills pitchers with punch. She is not a hostess or a waitress. Stacy is the somber wife of a company commander. Her husband, Rhett, leads a company of over three hundred men. Ten days ago, one of his men died, unexpectedly, of natural causes. Stacy is also a leader, and on this day she is overseeing the reception after the memorial service for Rhett's soldier. Stacy mingles with wives and soldiers, and consoles the widow who's holding one of her four children. It is not uncommon for Stacy to be found leading alongside her husband at Army functions. Her role is every bit as important as his to maintaining the fabric of the families in their company.

The leadership role wasn't always hers to fill; it came along with the promotion Rhett received when transferring to their new post. The position of Family Readiness Group (FRG) Leader and being a commander's wife go hand in hand. After nine years of service, Rhett had earned his company command. Their lives were forever changed. The birth of their baby boy was part of this change. "Marshall was ten days old when he left for Iraq." Rhett would take over his new position for a company that was already deployed. His first deployment would be for six months. "I feel fortunate that he wasn't gone the whole time. I think that's hard. Obviously, I'll be able to do it, but it gets hard when they miss so much," she says while glancing over to their son.

The Army was something Rhett always wanted to do. When Stacy met him in college, he was enrolled in ROTC, and was training to become an officer. In the early years of their marriage, Rhett spent many weeks away on countless training schools and officer courses. Stacy enjoyed her post-college career as a schoolteacher, teaching on base occasionally. They made friends and moved, made friends and moved. "You're in a wonderful environment because chances are if you walk up to a door there is someone who can relate to what you are going through." Stacy believes that reaching out to neighbors is a great way to get involved and to find support in the Army through moves and deployments. "I think making friends, and realizing that a lot of other people are in the same situation, you make good friends that way. The girl that used to live next door to me, I [would] talk to her a several times a week. She's at Fort Bragg now. I have another friend who is super close to me, and they're in Fort Polk now." Stacy's support of her neighbors goes beyond the normal cup of sugar. Last spring when her neighbor went into labor, Stacy was there for her. The mother-to-be was having her first child, and her husband was in Iraq. Stacy never hesitated to help. She knew it was a part of the unspoken rules of the Army wives' friendship.

Support in Stacy's life is a double-sided coin. For herself, she seeks family and close Army friends when Rhett is away. She plans trips to visit her family, friends, in-laws, whatever helps break up the time. There is an FRG support chain for every soldier and their family. But, there are people who seek more than support from her as the FRG leader. As Stacy explains, "It's a support network, and a way to get information out to spouses or family members. Really, it's hard, because some people think of FRG too much and want to rely on FRG too much." She believes that families set their expectations too high on the FRG. "I definitely want to make sure people know it's not a lawn service. It's not a baby-sitting service. It's strictly for information and to support the soldiers and families when they are gone." This side of her support role in the Army is one with its highs and lows from bake sales to funerals. And, unlike the average PTA, their information revolves around war.

The leadership role she fills for her company is one which carries many responsibilities. Officially, she is the primary source of information for the families of over three hundred soldiers. However, it is her unofficial duties, which fill most of her time while she raises Marshall. Today is one of those days, as she puts together the reception and helps console her friends.

Beyond the FRG, Stacy is involved in the Officer's Wives Club on post, as the historian. "I take pictures at all the events and scrapbook them." They plan and participate in events such as Oktoberfest, lunch-ins, and bowling. "I bowl every Tuesday morning, but I am a horrible bowler. It is fun. Last week, I was ecstatic. I bowled 166 for one of my games, and I barely ever break 100 so I was like, 'Wow.' It was a fluke." Her involvement is no fluke. It helps her to build relationships, which she can rely on during Rhett's next deployment to Iraq. The thought of war brings backs memories of the last time he was away.

"If I am waiting for a letter, or wanting mail, I will go through old letters. I will even go through letters we wrote when we were dating because I've kept all of those. And, of course, I save all my e-mails. Last year when they were gone, communication wasn't the best. When there was a dry spell I would just look at my old e-mails and read those instead."

Rhett was extremely busy leading his company. Finding time to call home was difficult Stacy says. She received "a little over a handful of phone calls the whole time." Like many who have been separated by this war, Stacy and Rhett relied on the Internet to communicate.

During the deployment Stacy traveled home to Wisconsin to visit with old friends. She sought help and companionship, but finds it is hard the longer they are in the Army to relate to those outside in the civilian world. "When I go home, I still have friends from college and high school. I love them to death, but their lives are completely different from mine. They can try to relate a little, but they can't. In some ways, they just don't understand." Rhett is the only person her friends in Wisconsin know in the service. "It is easier to be here (on base) some-times, because people around here understand. I think when I go back home my friends don't know what it is like for the families that are left behind, when they (the soldiers) are gone." Whether or not they understand what it means to live life in the Army, Stacy does feel a more positive change in the feelings of Americans towards the military itself.

"I have been impressed and surprised that people do think of us, and do think about the military now. I don't think that people used to think so much of the military and what the military is doing for them. I think since 9-11 people are thinking a lot differently and maybe are more appreciative of what they are doing for us and doing for our future."

Regardless of how the public or her friends and family feel towards her Army life, she is confident in their decisions, and what the future will bring them. Stacy knows the deep responsibilities that come with being an Army wife. Especially, because of her position as the FRG leader which gives her insight into the lives of hundreds of wives and their soldiers. She is modest about her personal role. Instead, she points to her husband as the one who carries the many burdens.

"There is not enough money in the world for these guys. They are not getting paid well. Rhett works thirteen, fourteen hours a day most of the time. That is crazy to me. He has things that he enjoys and he would love to do more often if he had more time. He loves biking, but he hasn't been able to do it since he's been in command. [For example], he went hunting last weekend, he got called in, and had to come in and do paper work. On Saturday morning."

His long hours translate into minimal time with their son. Like most toddlers nearing the age of two, Marshall has an early bedtime. "Right now, he works really late hours. He doesn't get home, some nights, until eight or eight-thirty, and Marshall is already in bed. He's gone before we even get up [in the morning]." The last year and a half of Stacy's life has come with dramatic changes. Besides the biggest change, motherhood, she has become a "mother" to the company wives and families. When the next transition comes, the next deployment, the next funeral, the next meeting, she will fill her role standing right alongside her husband. Being Rhett's wife is the most important role she has.

Samantha

Listening to Daddy's Bear

Samantha

She's been called an Army brat. Her father spent most of his adult life serving and, eventually, retired from the Army years ago. The term "brat" simply refers to time spent as a child trying to grow up in an ever-changing Army home. Samantha does not shy from her childhood past. Samantha reevaluates that title now that it is given to her own child. She looks at her own baby, Ella, cuddled in her arms, and thinks her daughter's childhood may end up being similar to hers. She is now a wife and a mother raising a family under the hand of the Army.

Becoming a soldier's wife, which is usually so foreign and new to wives, was more like wrapping herself in the security blanket she had known all her life. Maybe, she always knew she would find a soldier to marry. Maybe, she wanted to marry a man who reminded her of her father, who has passed away. Fate and faith, it seemed, had landed her right in the arms of her husband, Ryan. Set up originally to become pen pals, she met Ryan in person only weeks before he was going on his first tour to Kuwait. He was one of the most handsome men she had ever seen and Samantha's heart fluttered with each meeting as his deployment date approached. "We were inseparable for two weeks." It was an instant connection, a blossoming friendship that wouldn't be allowed to wither simply because of war.

> "He called me all the time. He would take a phone card and run it up, and then go and charge it again. We said, 'I love you,' over the phone. I didn't like having him gone. We were just concentrating on getting to know one another, and he likes to talk. It just felt right."

For the six months Ryan was gone, they courted through letters, e-mails, and phone calls. Their romance had grown, and Ryan was sure Samantha was "the one." Shortly after returning from Kuwait, he prepared himself for a big proposal production. First stop was Samantha's mother's school, where she worked as a secretary, to ask permission. Dressed in his freshly pressed Army Dress Blues, he entered the school. "All the kids thought he was George Washington. I later found out that he had brought my engagement ring and asked my mom to be his

Mother-in-law." After being given the go ahead from her mother, Ryan continued with his plot to give Samantha the surprise of her life. However, Ryan was slightly unprepared as he picked her up from work.

> "He only had a pair of long underwear to use as a blind fold. He said, 'I promise they're clean.' Finally, after a long drive he said, 'Okay, you can take it off. You can open your eyes.' I looked up and we were standing in the middle of the Kansas State stadium on the fifty-yard line. He got down on one knee on the Wildcat (logo). I said, 'Yes! Oh, yes!' Then we got in the car and he said a prayer."

Samantha says that Ryan is one of the biggest football fans she has ever known. His upstairs office can attest to the fact, it is covered in college football paraphernalia. While in Iraq he made sure to get a glimpse of the playoffs whenever he could.

Their plans for a summer wedding were quickly changed by the needs of the Army. Ryan was going to Iraq. Samantha was heartbroken and physically shaken at her new husband's absence. He left only weeks after a ceremony shared with family and friends.

> "He was gone for a year. That was hard, because we had just gotten married. We had been married five weeks. I had lived with my mom until we got married. I had never lived by myself. It was kind of cool, because I decorated the apartment and got to be independent. I went to school and I went to work and I took care of everything. I was figuring out the military thing from the wife's point of view and not the kid's. It was hard. There were a few times when I would go into my closet to a find [one of his] shirts for church. I could still smell him on his clothes and I would find myself sitting on the closet floor crying, and I didn't make it to church. It's like they always say, 'The first year of marriage is the toughest,' and I thought, 'Yeah, when you're there all by yourself for a year.'"

Life was dramatically changing for Samantha. Her experience as an Army brat had always been a sheltered one; her father was rarely in danger in his twenty plus years of service. When he was away, it was her mother who helped their family; she was the strong one. Now, it was Samantha's turn to be the wife, the one who stayed behind.

Her strengths in this position would be challenged as his year in Iraq continued. Ryan experienced many close calls. "They went to a mine field and they were marking land mines. He stepped on one, and it didn't go off." His position guaranteed that he would be working in an office building. Only weeks after leaving his post, the building in which he had spent so many hours was bombed. Later there was another close call. "Someone [in his company] was shot in the face by a sniper. He went out to the roof top with his Captain to look for the sniper, and his Captain was shot in the leg." The stories and the danger Ryan faced on a daily basis fueled the difficulties of daily life for his new bride.

Samantha thought of Ryan constantly. The holidays were an especially difficult time. Ryan's love for Christmas stayed in Samantha's heart, and in her living room. "I left the Christmas tree up. It was driving me nuts. I was itching to put it away, but he loves Christmas so much and I wanted him to see the little tree that I had decorated. So, we had Christmas with his mom and dad in March." After their belated celebration Samantha asked her husband if she could finally take down the tree. It had stood there for nearly four months, decorated in love, but a constant reminder that Ryan was away for the holidays. He wasn't there to share their first Christmas as husband and wife.

The year was over; Ryan was coming home. They would celebrate by taking a proper honeymoon abroad, something that Ryan's work schedule had prevented before. Samantha had been saving for months. With their honeymoon adventure behind them, they focused on what would be the beginning of their family. Samantha was pregnant with their first baby, a girl, due in the spring. Spring was also the time Ryan's unit would be returning to Iraq. "This time when he left, I was eight months pregnant, and that was kind of rough. I wasn't looking forward to it. When you're married and you don't feel well (during pregnancy), you want your husband. He's your comfort now." Her mother was able to help her through the birth, and baby Ella was born early, but very healthy. "It was nice that my mom was there. I wasn't alone like some women." A little version of her husband had arrived in the world. "When she was born she came out looking like Ryan. Now, she looks at me with his expressions, and she has his little temper." Soon Ryan would be able to hold the tiny version of himself.

"When she was five weeks old he came home, and he got to see her. He walked in, and he said, 'You must be my little girl.' He was holding her and looking at her, and everything. We were a family." Ryan was home for his two week "R and R." Priority is usually given to soldiers who have births of dependents while away, and his commanders were able to get him home quickly to see his baby Ella. He held her every waking moment. And in those few moments he did sleep, he held Samantha instead.

The two weeks went by quickly. Samantha would return to her phone and computer to update her husband on Ella's daily progress and adventures. He made phone calls when he could. For a time he averaged a ten minute morale call a few times a week, which comforted Samantha, and gave Ella the chance to learn her father's voice over the phone. Mostly, they grew as a family over the Internet. Samantha would receive an e-mail daily to which she would reply. Often she sent the newest pictures of his baby girl rolling over or making a silly baby face.

"She keeps me busy but, at the same time, Ryan's missing all this stuff and when she does something I want to tell him. I write him at night, like, 'She sat up today and she did this today and we've got teeth coming in'. I'll tell him when he calls, but he's still not the first to know." Many moments bring her deep frustrations and sadness. Samantha begins to think, "I'm done. I'm done. I didn't get married to be alone. This was not how it's supposed to be. He should be here with me." Those countless minutes, hours, and days without Ryan make her question their future. She knows he, after eight years of service, has a deep love for the Army. And for herself, "The Army is somewhat of a security blanket. I'm used to it. Part of me wants him to stay in, and part of me doesn't. He doesn't like being deployed all the time. He doesn't like missing a year of his daughter's life. I don't think he should be making a decision right now."

With their future plans for their life in the Army put on hold, Samantha focuses on the day-to-day tasks of being a new mom. They long to be a complete family, together again. In a couple months, he will return to his loving wife and his little girl. Ella will almost be one. Even with the many months away from her father, "She'll know his voice," Samantha says confidently. She brings Ella one of her favorite toys, a brown teddy bear. Samantha holds them both in her arms as she pushes a button inside the bear. Ella's face lights up as her daddy's voice comes from within her teddy. Samantha glances up, reflecting on her time as an Army wife.

> "If you really love somebody, you do it. There's not a method. There's not a book or guidelines. You take care of the baby and the house; you take care of everything. And you count the days until he comes home. That's what being married and being in love is all about."

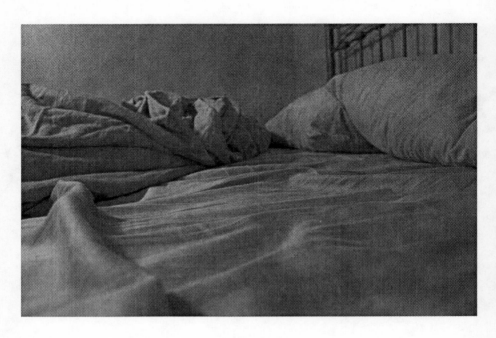

Empty Bed

Nighttime

When your soldier is away,
nighttime can turn into
the most difficult time.
It means lying in bed,
alone.

What once felt crowded,
occupied by a strong soldier's body,
fought over space and covers,
is now vast and empty.
What once was intimate,
for sharing with a spouse, is now,
simply,
a lonely piece of furniture.

Deeper, and deeper,
you burrow your head into the pillow.
You toss and turn.
Sleep.
Sleep.
I need to go to sleep.
Why can't I just sleep?

Loneliness overwhelms you.
Your covers feel heavy,
they smother you.
There is darkness.

The emptiness of the room consumes you.
You turn and face the empty side of your bed.

Do you dare to reach out your arm and feel the cold,
clean spot that was left behind?
Do you dare to run your fingers over the sheets,
void of the person they are meant to cover?

Nighttime is a lonely time.
While the world sleeps,
you stay awake.
You lay in waiting,
in waking,
for minutes,
and then hours.
Forced into a state of exhaustion,
and exacerbated from your sadness,
you lay tired and awake.

Check the cell phone one last time,
to make sure it is charged, and in the 'on' position.
Lay back down.

Light through the bedroom window shines on you.
You begin to study the room,
the shadows on the wall.
You stretch out your hand,
and study its curves,
until you see *it*.

You begin rubbing it with your thumb,
turning it just so it shines in the dim light.
The gold and stones are so smooth and flawless.
Tears well in your eyes.
The wetness rolls down your cheek,
onto your pillow,
saturating the softness
as a thousand tears have before.
You close them once,
then twice,
then fall quietly asleep.

Finally, in your dreams,
the bed is whole once again,
and you are held all night long.

Peace.

Part 3

Getting Out and Loving It

Woman who will be leaving the Army upon completion of their husband's contract

Laura

Steven's Carved Pumpkin

Laura

Laura is in tears. The UHAUL parked outside their Army quarters is already too full to fit anymore of their belongings. She and the house are in distress. Moving was never easy for her. Her children try to help. They get the mail one last time, they help their daddy pack the already overly packed van, and her youngest cuddles in mama's lap. What was her life for so many years will be a distant memory in her rear view mirror as she drives away through the post gate. Her husband, Steven, has turned in his equipment. His time is done. During this era of war his unit left a crack open, for only a couple of weeks, to let soldiers slip through and out of the Army if their contract was up. Otherwise, soldiers like Steven would be forced to stay in due to stop-loss and deploy. Steven was out.

Months ago, it was a very different picture. The future was completely unknown. Laura would wait daily to hear word if Steven would be able to get out of the Army or be sent back to Iraq. She was neither optimistic nor pessimistic, simply frustrated. Frustrated at the Army and angered at what was going on with her husband and her family since Steven's return from Iraq. For Laura the complexity of the situation is overwhelming. She talks to his first sergeant on a consistent basis, begging, sometimes ordering that Steven be let out.

Laura wasn't always in such a desperate situation. Her time as an Army wife is unique, in part, because she has done it twice. On two separate occasions she has married into the Army. She married her first husband when she was seventeen; he was already in the Army, while she was in high school. They were married for four years, all spent in the Army. They had two daughters together, born at Fort Hood, during some of the most trying months of her life. Life in Killeen, Texas was difficult. "Anywhere that was cheap enough for you to live in was in a really bad neighborhood." They were on the on post housing waiting list for over three years. Ironically, when they arrived at their next post, Fort Hood housing was finally available.

It was at their next post that their relationship turned for the worse. Life at home was unbearable. Some of her most joyful moments were when she and her previous husband invited the single soldiers in his unit over for dinner. "We fed them once a month. They called it 'feeding the homeless,' because you know how chow hall food can only be so good for so long." One soldier in particular, Steven, stood out to Laura. He would always stay to help clean the dishes after the meal was finished. As her current relationship withered, she desired to be with Steven and to have a better life for her and her daughters. Adultery in the Army is against the law for both parties involved. A soldier who is involved with a married soldier's spouse can be prosecuted, fined, imprisoned, and kicked out of the Army.

> "My ex-husband got out [of the Army] when we divorced. He used me, pretty much. He told me that he wouldn't get Steven in trouble with the Army if, when he filed for divorce, I gave him full custody of the girls, so that he could get out of the Army. [I] ended up having to go to court because he refused me custody back. But, they lived with me. So, we went back to court and I got custody. He didn't even show up to court."

Her ex-husband is currently serving in the Air National Guard. Their daughters visit him regularly during school breaks.

Shortly after her divorce, Laura and Steven married. They began to try for their own addition to the family. For many months they tried to get pregnant and even sought fertility testing. Eventually, Laura's belly began to grow; they were expecting a baby boy. This would be Steven's first child and, because of medical conditions, his only child. Their happiness was overturned by the thirty-day notice given to his unit for the pending deployment to Iraq. Steven would be gone for the remainder of her pregnancy and the birth. When Steven deployed they had been married just two years.

"He missed the whole [birth] experience. I sent him pictures. My friend Carrie, God bless her, she took pictures while I was in labor. So, he saw pictures of the whole thing, because in a military hospital they won't let you videotape." They named him Noah. He would have to wait to meet his daddy when he came home on "R and R." "I have pictures there of the first time he held him," Laura says glancing up at a family photo collage on the wall. "[It] was at the airport. He was all giddy. He was so excited. The whole time he was home he held him." Laura was overjoyed at the sight of her husband holding their son for the first time. She wanted to cherish and hold onto that moment forever. Forever was postponed as his two weeks ended and he returned to Iraq to complete the yearlong tour.

Laura's body and soul yearned for Steven to be near her. She missed him, but more so, she worried about him. The war's toll was hurting the strong character of a husband she loved. He had many close calls. On their anniversary Laura waited by the phone for a loving call, but the phone never rang. Steven was involved in a firefight for nearly two hours on that day. "He spent our anniversary being shot at." Just to recall the story upsets her, and physically affects her to this day.

"I didn't talk to him [very] much while he was in Iraq. Sometimes, it would be three weeks until I would hear from him." While he was gone, she remembers the morning time as being the most stressful time of the day. Six o'clock to be exact. "We were told if something happens to your soldier someone would be at your door at six o'clock in the morning. If he was killed." She began to fear any outside contact during that early morning hour. If her phone would ring she would ignore it in fear and simply lay on her bed denying the possibility that anything bad could have happened to him. Steven's tour, though dangerous, left him virtually unharmed. He retuned safely to her arms and to the arms of his new son.

> "Steven [finally] came home, Noah had only actually seen him in a picture. I had a picture of Steven in his DCU's that I kept in Noah's room on the wall. When he [arrived], Steven tried to hold him and [Noah] didn't let him. He was like, 'Who are you?' We got home and he saw the picture of daddy. I was holding him and he [looked] at the picture and looked at Steven (in his DCU's), and recognized like, 'Oh okay, I know who you are now.' He went right to Steven. They've been inseparable ever since. He knew who he was when he saw the picture."

Steven's tour in Iraq was a turning point for Laura in many regards. Although the toll of war was a constant battle during the year he was away, it has been the reaction to war in him and their family, which has solidified her anger towards the Army. "He came back with anger issues. He was angry with a lot of stuff and he suppressed those feelings long enough. You're going to blow up and hurt somebody you love."

> "[What] made the decision for him to get out is PTSD (Post Traumatic Stress Disorder). He's affected by that badly because [of what] he saw. You're never going to be the same after you spend time in a war. It has really affected his mental state. You can't take him in public without him making a comment about someone of Middle Eastern decent. The Army is not doing anything about it."

Steven has been prescribed a daily medication for his PTSD, but has yet to be offered a chance to see a mental health professional. His usual appointment lasts just long enough to write down the prescription for a refill, nothing more. Laura is frustrated by the lack of treatment for her husband and other soldiers after their return from the combat zone. "It is not what it used to be, people don't care. You know, they are going over there and changing people's lives forever and not doing anything about it." The life changing experience of war for her husband has had many life changing effects on herself. Not only has she lost respect for the Army, but she has also begun taking antidepressants and anxiety medications to help calm her nerves. "The depression stuff from him rubs off on me. I feel sad because there is nothing that I can do to make him feel better. That makes you feel like you are lacking as a wife because you can't make it better for him." She feels like she would take just about anything to help her get through the next few months, an illusion to make time and pain go away until they get out of the Army.

The decision to try to leave the Army was not any easy one. "He had planned to go career. He was all 'Hooah. Hooah.' Then [his new unit] just really ruined it because they have no pride in their soldiers. It's the lack of pride. He says that the Army is changing. It's not what it used to be. People look at it as if it is a free ride, and it's not. There's no pride anymore." Her opinion stems from the difficult time Steven has while in Iraq and what she hears on post from day to day.

> "I have a lot of pride in Steven. I'm very proud of what my husband does, but it's hard to keep him motivated and happy when you go to work everyday and people act like high schoolers, like children. That's what they are, a bunch of eighteen year olds that don't care. I think that's what we've really lost. The deployment was what really made us lose our pride in the military, because he went through a lot of stuff with the guys he was with over there. They were like high school kids making fun of him because he's short, and doing stuff like that. It's immature and it's childish. You can't get away from it. I don't know why. Maybe [it's because] everyone is so young. There's just so much drama. You lose your pride when people are constantly talking about how bad it is. Don't get me wrong, the military hasn't been bad. I've had three kids and didn't pay a dime for it. I have great medical coverage. I can say that my husband served in Iraq and, no, it's not something that he wanted to do and not something that he wants to do again. You have to experience it to know why. I don't know. I don't hate it, but I don't love it anymore. Not like I used to."

If Steven were to stay in the Army he would be on his way back to Iraq in less than a year. The scheduled deployment fills her in fear. It would be the second survival, the second round of hardship, on him and their family. "He doesn't want to go back, because he counts himself lucky that he made it back this time." Steven fears the physical aspects of war. Laura's mind anticipates the harsh mental and emotional toll a second tour would take on her husband.

> "If he goes back [to Iraq] I get scared that my husband will never come back. Maybe he won't die, but it will change him more, and he's already half of what he once was. My husband used to smile and joke and have a good time. He doesn't smile any more, he's not happy. He's not who he was when he left, and I don't want him to come back again even more depressed and stressed out."

Laura shares the pictures Steven brought back from Iraq. Her living room floor is scattered with a barrage of scrap-booking supplies. Stickers, patches, newspaper clippings, mementos, and, most importantly, photographs flood her carpet. This isn't a new project. Laura thoughtfully finishes each page revealing powerful moments during Steven's time in Iraq. She knows that the pictures and the pages mean more to him everyday. She points to the pictures on a page in a large green scrapbook with a gold Army insignia on the front. "To help him deal with it. That's why I put the vehicle that killed friends of his. He was a part of the clean-up crew that had to clean that up and he took pictures of it for a reason. Those are his pictures and he did it for a reason. So, I want him to know that it is okay to look at them." Laura shares an unspoken understanding with her husband and his need to own and view photographs from his time in Iraq.

> "My mom works at a Wal-Mart photo studio down in Texas and the National Guard has just returned there. She has had a lot of people that have brought in pictures that, by Wal-Mart standards, they are not supposed to print. My mom mentioned it to me one time and I told her that you couldn't *not* do it. And she asked me, 'Why?' And I said, 'It's how these soldiers deal with what they went through. It may take years, but at least they'll have the pictures to look back and go, 'You know, it's okay to be angry. It's okay to be sad and stuff like that.' And my mom, since then, has been printing the pictures that the soldiers bring in."

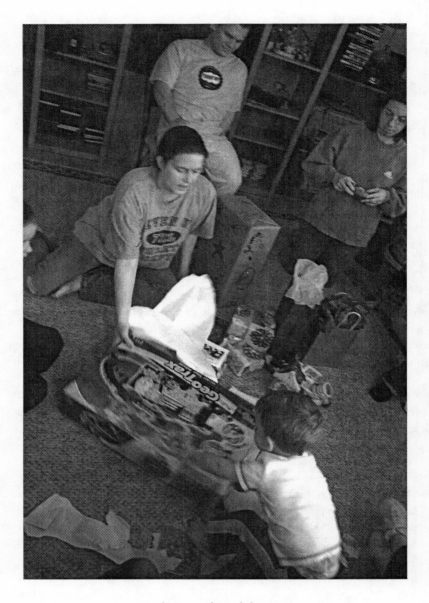

Noah's Second Birthday Party

Jenny

Hugging Doggie Bear
Jenny and Katie

"The longer it goes on, the more attached she is to me.
She just won't let me out of her sight."
– Jenny

Jenny

Katie is glued to her mother's leg while holding her toy, "Doggie Bear." Katie barely lets her mother out of her sight to do simple things, even use the restroom. As much as Jenny adores her four-year-old daughter, she cannot wait for this time to be over. She knows that Katie's anxiety filled arms will soon let her go, once her father, Thomas, returns from war. Her tiny frame will cling to her father again and Jenny will have peace in her life and in her heart. Too young to express much emotion, Katie is drawn to her mother for every comfort she desires. Jenny's eyes well up thinking back to his first deployment. "She (Katie) realized that he was gone, but after the first few weeks it didn't seem to bother her that much."

Katie's outward actions speak volumes of what a difficult time this is in her life. Her daddy, who she practices push-ups with on the living room floor, has been taken from her, again. She was just eighteen months old the first time he left for Iraq. Jenny raised her into her twos in a house they bought just five weeks before he left. It was a time filled with change. Jenny and her family had just returned to the states after living in Germany with Thomas' first unit. Jenny was never happy about her husband's decision to join the Army; Germany was a compromise. She had taken German in high school, and looked forward to living abroad in a country where she could understand the language.

"Six months or so after we got married he decided to join the National Guard, and I was not happy about it. I was *really* unhappy about it. My parents are kind of pacifists, I guess you would say. They are opposed to war for just about any reason. They're not militant. They're not real super vocal about it, but we did hear about it. My dad got drafted right after my parents got married. He ended up going to Korea for about a year. We heard his stories, and my dad is just one of these rebellious types. He refused to salute a particular officer because he thought he didn't deserve to be saluted. So, we heard Dad's anti-military stories."

What Thomas always had in the back of his mind as a great career path, Jenny was deeply against. Coming from a long lineage of military service, Thomas expected to join, and his passion for the military expanded as he studied history in college. His degree would be necessary to become an officer. Jenny and Thomas married shortly after attending the same college. They originally met at a church camp in high school in North Central Wyoming. After joining the National Guard, Thomas got even more serious about the Army, and went into Active Duty. "He didn't [convince me]. He just did it."

The first year of their marriage was a difficult time. Jenny was reluctant to adjust to the Army life. "[After he joined] he was gone every summer. I was like, 'Don't you want to be with me? Why would you take a job where you would be away?'" There was nothing fair about the Army life and nothing agreeable about being away from the one she loved. The Army did provide for her and Thomas, though. At their first post, in Germany, Jenny was surprised by the income they received. "People talk about Lieutenants not making any money, but I mean the minute he went on Active Duty, we had way more money than either of us was ever used to." Giving less and less thought to money, Jenny grew in her enjoyment of the Army life, particularly her time in Germany.

Jenny has recreated the German experience with authentic German furniture purchased at a second hand store. A traditional folk art coo-coo clock hangs on the wall, marking the hours. Even so, Jenny most important treasure came in the form of her daughter, Katie.

> "I was really, really sick when I was pregnant the first trimester. I just moved from the bed to the couch everyday. I was just so sick. I couldn't keep anything down, and I was really weak. He would come home to find little cans of food I had tried to eat around, where [instead] he's used to coming home and finding me cooking dinner and the house picked up."

Fortunately, Thomas was around nearly the entire pregnancy to help Jenny through the trials of those nine months. Katie's birth was a small celebration and it wouldn't be until months later that she would meet many of her grandparents and extended family. After three years in Germany, they returned to the states, and following a brief training period, they received his orders to join a unit already in combat. Jenny was heartbroken. It was one of the hardest things she has had to do as an Army wife and she has her regrets. "The move followed by the deployment was the hardest thing, and this was a bad place to buy [the house] too. As far as the church [goes], I mean, we're not even in the city [the church is in]." A new mother, in a new town, trying to put together their new house, she used the Internet to talk to Thomas daily to help her deal with her stress. Katie was much too young to understand what was happening.

Thomas was initially excited about serving in war. He went with the usual high described by first time war veterans. During his first tour he had a special painting made for Jenny done by an Iraqi artist. She points to a large framed painting in her foyer. "He had that done from a photo in Iraq the first time [he was there]. I'm not crazy about it." Jenny finds the gesture thoughtful, however. Thomas was actually trying to emulate a similar painting hanging in Jenny's parents' home. "My dad had it done in Korea. My parents had this big painting of their wedding picture over their fireplace, and I thought 'Oh, how neat.' Then he sent that home, but it doesn't look like us." When she looks over at the large portrait she can barely see herself, but it represents an important time in their relationship. Although the painting was created from a photograph of Jenny and Thomas at an Army formal, it is really a reminder of the distance they once experienced. A distance they can reflect back on once they leave the Army.

Thomas is serving in his second tour in Iraq and Jenny says her husband is tired. "He's tired of being away." Jenny's eyes carry those same emotions. Eyes that show she is exhausted from being alone and longing to be whole again. This second tour has been much different. Katie is well aware of her father's absence in their lives. "She'll draw him pictures to send whenever we send a box. Sometimes when we are chatting in the morning she'll type a bunch of numbers or letters or she'll type her name. He can tell [it's her], so then he says, 'Hey, Katie.'"

"[We] send packages every three to four weeks. Katie always sends him packages of gum. That's what he asks for, gum and Kool-Aid. I always send him his [hunting] magazines. It never fails, as soon as I send a package, another one (magazine) comes." It is hard to ignore Thomas' hunting enthusiasm. Just inside their front door and a wild turkey's feathers and claws are displayed alongside the skins and heads of other animals.

It has been nearly seven years of service for their family and when Thomas returns in less than two months they will begin the path to leave the Army. Thomas is an officer, and does not fall under the "stop-loss" policy. The military life was never Jenny's desired path. Outsiders have a hard time empathizing with their situation, and it can be frustrating at times.

"In the military community people are pretty smart. Generally, people around here have some familiarity, but where we went to college, people don't understand. They'd be like, 'I can't believe the Army does this to you.' Well, that's not helping, thank you. When he came home on leave, he was wearing his uniform, and we had to pick him up. And everybody wanted to shake his hand and thank him. We're like, 'Hello, we haven't seen each other in six months.' The Vietnam generation got spit on [and] they were called 'baby killers.' So, I guess it's better than that."

Jenny looks forward to the days when they will live free of the Army. Mostly, she is focused on Thomas returning safely from Iraq. "The longer it goes on, the more attached she (Katie) is to me. She just won't let me out of her sight." Along with the health and well-being of her daughter, Jenny knows how much better she will feel when Thomas is safe at home. She can hardly talk about his absence in her own life. "She (Katie) brings it up," Jenny says, quivering with sadness and longing for her husband. "We just say that we miss him and that he'll be home." As her eyes well up, she tells the sweet story of how Katie and Thomas share their gum from thousands of miles apart. In each package Katie sends her daddy she includes his favorite gum. "When he writes back he puts a piece of gum in his letters." Then Thomas and Katie can chew together.

Alicia

Tickling Alicia

*"It's so hard. Not only on the military soldier,
but on the spouse and his family.
I mean, there's a lot of pressure.
There's a lot of stress and there's very little appreciation for everything that they do.
It deserves more respect than it actually gets."
-Alicia*

Alicia

Alicia is angry with the Army. Her husband Craig is a broken soldier, and should not have to return to Iraq. She was so distraught over the news of another deployment that she became physically ill, blacking out while at work. She is overcome with fear and frustration, and overwhelmed by what the future may bring, when Craig leaves for war once again.

Alicia met Craig when she was in high school. "It was pretty much like small town boy meets girl." They were from two tiny towns thirteen miles apart in Northern California. They married a few years ago while in college, and shortly afterwards Craig decided to join the Army. Alicia was far from thrilled, and attempted to talk him out of the decision. Craig comes from a family rich in military history, his father had served in Vietnam, along with other relatives. "That's why there really was no talking him out of it, because where we're from, a town of two thousand; it's hard to get out of small town life. So, he wanted to come join the military for a couple of years, kind of travel around, and then that would leave us financially stable enough to start our own life. He never wanted to do career military. He just wanted to join and do it."

Craig went to boot camp with his brother (who is now a Purple Heart recipient). Alicia was sick without him, and fell into a depression. She didn't eat for days. When she saw him at the airport upon completion of his training she was so excited, she toppled him over, leaping over bags, and dodging around passengers. Their first duty station was a three-day drive from their family and friends in California. Alicia has had a difficult time being so far from her family. She is a triplet, and has never spent such an extensive amount of time away from her siblings. She hates being alone, and never experienced an empty house until Craig was sent to Iraq.

While away on tour, Alicia lived alone for the first time. She attempted to keep herself busy, but fell into a deep sadness while he was away, collapsing in tears on many occasions. "I would just curl up on my floor and cry. I probably cried, on average, once a day, sometimes twice." She felt trapped, unable to travel home to see family. Alicia feels that people don't understand how difficult it is for Craig to be away. Her longing for companionship eats away at her with each day of his absence.

Alicia has always known that Craig would likely have to deploy, but she did not anticipate the obstacles they would face. Craig experienced medical problems as the lymph nodes on his body swelled up. It made life as a soldier a daily challenge; the fifty pounds of gear would pound the swollen areas of his body until it was too difficult for him to perform even simple tasks. He was sent in for x-rays, and was eventually evacuated to Germany because the Army believed he might have had cancer. The biopsy came back negative for cancer, but his condition was a mystery. Alicia was told by the Army medical staff that they were going to send him to the states, to Maddigan at Fort Lewis, Washington or The Brooke Army Medical Center at Fort Sam Houston, Texas to diagnose and treat his condition.

> "Well, they messed up their tickets and sent him back to Iraq without ever fixing what was wrong. He did the rest to of his year there, came home still having the problem. We're constantly taking him to doctors and saying, 'Hey, what's going on?' [His] lymph nodes are swelling; it's to the point where he can't put his arms down to his side because it hurts him. They swell up here (pointing to her sides) when he has his rucksack on. His "full battle rattle" hurts him. Whatever happened to him, it happened in Iraq. He didn't have this problem before."

The initial trip to Germany for diagnosis was one of the worst days in Alicia's life. Information got out to the Family Readiness Group that he was evacuated, but for the wrong reason. Her commander's wife informed her that Craig had been involved in a firefight. The wife told her that he was most likely dead. "I lost it. I pretty much went into a zombie state for a couple of days." Believing that her husband was dead, Alicia was devastated. A couple days later, Craig called her from his hospital bed in Germany, and she began to shed tears at the very sound of his voice. She told him why she was reacting in such a way, and he grew furious. Alicia is angry with the Army because there was no action. "Nothing was ever done." The repercussions from the experience of hearing that Craig was killed still haunt her. This pain is one of the reasons that she cannot bare to see him leave for war again.

During his tour, Craig did not reveal very much to Alicia about his daily life as a Scout, one of the more dangerous jobs in the Army. He knew that telling her too much while he was still on foreign soil would only scare her more. Upon his return he began to slowly reveal details. Some stories come from difficult moments, like the morning he put on his combat boots, and Alicia looked down to see blood spatter. He had to tell her whose blood was on his boots. Other stories display some of the few humorous moments in war. Once, he was riding in a Humvee and was hit by a pigeon. "He was traveling fifty-five miles an hour in one direction and the bird was going about five miles an hour in the other. Bam! They collided. He was hit right in the head, and began shouting to the other soldiers, 'I got hit! I got hit!' Then he looked up to see feathers everywhere. His claim to fame was that the pigeons were smarter than the Iraqis, because they actually got him." Craig had many stories to tell his wife, as do most soldiers, but he only shared those with a fun or happy ending, on the phone or by e-mail while still in Iraq.

Upon his return life didn't automatically jump back to the way it once was. Alicia knew things would never be the same for them. War followed him and in his dreams he would return to battle. For months, Alicia would be scared to join him in bed if he had already fallen asleep. Craig admits that the war torments him at night, and when Alicia gets into bed, sometimes he thinks that she is an Iraqi, and is ready to fight. Alicia has learned to wake him before he gets violent and that it is best to leave the room to avoid her husband's nightmares. Of course, these violent dreams have made Craig feel terrible, and they have sought counseling.

The time after a deployment is called "stabilization" in the Army. It is a time for soldiers and their families to get the help they need, such as rest and counseling, before the Army relocates them or deploys them again. During Craig's stabilization, they sought out an Army marriage counselor to help them, and they recommend doing so to other couples. It was a positive experience for them because it taught Craig how to open up about war and taught Alicia how to listen. He learned how to make the transition back into her world. For Alicia, the counseling became a great asset, and eventually things grew more normal, even at night.

The months following Craig's stabilization became a trying time for Alicia, both physically and mentally. She was diagnosed with cancer and had to undergo surgery. It was devastating for her to discover that at the age of twenty-one she would have to undergo a surgery that might possibly prevent her from ever having children. It took some time, but Craig was able to be there for her. "When I was going in for surgery, my husband had to sit there and convince people that he could come to my appointment." The surgery was successful, but Alicia fears the future. The cancer could return. The surgery not only drained her emotionally, but physically. She was unable to walk for days. Craig's redeployment will leave her alone should she have the surgery again.

"One of the things I'm concerned about is that they have to monitor the cancer for a year before they can say, 'Okay, we're pretty sure it's not coming back.' So, if I end up having cancer while he's gone, if it comes back while he's gone; that, for one, is absolutely going to devastate me because then I will have no one. I will have to go into the surgery and do it all over again, and I will have to do it by myself."

With both of their medical conditions, she believes that there is no reason why he should have to return to war. She is distraught because he still has the lymph node problem. "There is no reason why my husband should have to go back to Iraq at this point. They can't figure out what's wrong with him from the first time." Alicia also believes that they should take into account her own medical problem and the seriousness of cancer. "I just wish that they'd understand, and that's what irritates me so much about the military. They don't understand that there are special cases for everything."

Alicia hates to think about Craig leaving again. He is scheduled to leave in the coming months, and it is not going to be an easy time. "I'm very attached to my husband. We do everything together. We're still in the honeymoon stage. It's harder for me than it is for most wives." Alicia recognizes that the Army life is not something that she is cut out for doing her entire life. "I will stick it out and I love my husband. For as long as he is in the military and he has to be, I will stick it out. But, I am not military wife material." She gives those who can handle the lifestyle great credit and believes that others should too.

"It's so hard, not only on the military soldier, but on the spouse, and his family. I mean, there's a lot of pressure, there's a lot of stress and there's very little appreciation for everything that they do. It deserves more respect than it actually gets."

The deployments, training separations, and long daily hours have gotten to her. Craig typically works a seventeen to eighteen hour day, which Alicia says, puts a lot of strain on their marriage and on her. Their difficult life in the Army will likely be extended until after the next deployment. Alicia looks forward to a day and time when she no longer fears for Craig's safety each day.

"There is nothing harder than waking up everyday knowing your husband could be dead and you don't know it. It's a hard reality. I, honest to God, believe military wives don't get enough credit for this, at least the faithful ones. Every single day you have to go on. It's the hardest thing to do, to plan your husband's funeral while they're here. Who wants to have a conversation with a twenty-two year old guy, 'Where do you want to be buried?'"

Flipping the Bill

*"There is no reason why my husband should have
to go back to Iraq at this point.
They can't figure out what's wrong with him from the first time."*
-Alicia

Part 4

Married to a "Lifer"

Wives who believe that they will be in the Army until their husband retires with a minimum twenty years in service

Nicole

Holding Jay

Nicole

Content. Carefree. Casual. These are all words that describe Nicole. Today she exemplifies all of these qualities as she holds her infant son, Jay, and talks to her husband, Curtis. Little Jay looks like a precious doll nestled in her tall frame. He is pacifying himself as he falls quietly asleep. Nicole has been overjoyed with her son for the few months he has been in their lives. Jay was a homecoming baby, a symbol of her husband's return from his first tour in Iraq. She speaks about Iraq casually. It is not a difficult subject for her, even though Curtis is on his way back to Iraq. Nicole deliberately motions to the many framed photographs of her and Curtis and also Jay circling her living room.

"When he is all the way over there, it's hard, [but then again] there he is. Look up, there he is. I mean, look around my house. I wake up, there you (Curtis) are. It's kind of the same with him. When he left the first time, he made a pillowcase and had my picture on the pillowcase. There were pictures and letters and e-mails. We had stacks and stacks of letters."

Nicole and Curtis met casually, in a Wal-Mart parking lot one evening, while she was on her way out for the night with a group of her girl friends. She was the most beautiful and laid back girl he had met. Curtis was soon in love. He was attending college and she was finishing high school; it was young love, but it was also a very serious love. As her husband sits next to her, Nicole recalls how their engagement came about. "He proposed the second month we were together," Nicole says, as her husband disagrees and corrects her. "Oh, okay, the first month; on Valentine's Day."

"Everybody knew, but me [about the engagement]. It was a big surprise, a very big surprise. I was like, 'Are you serious?' When my mom got a look [at me], she said, 'What is that on your hand?' I'm the oldest. I'm the oldest girl of four kids."

Nicole was in love, but not ready to be married. She quickly said, 'Yes,' but with one stipulation. They would not get married until she was at least twenty-one. At the time she was eighteen, applying for college, and planning for life, but not ready to be a wife.

Curtis began weighing his own future. He had been supporting himself to make ends meet with his part-time job at McDonald's, but he knew that everything would change once they were married. Nicole also attended college and, in her junior year, Curtis surprised her with his career changing decision. "He thought it would be better to join the Army." She was genuinely content with his decision. Although she knew that there would be separation ahead of them, it was a choice that she supported him in.

As his time in service continued, so did the amount of time she was separated from Curtis. Following his basic and individual training he was sent to Germany for his first duty station. Soon she left school to be close to him. "It was different. The weather was funny, sunny one day, then snow the next day, but it was good. It was nice." She had moved to Germany and began living with some of his relatives who had a home not far from base. It was the perfect time for her to see a new place and enjoy a new culture. Everything up to that point had been carefree about her Army experience.

Curtis received a stateside assignment and they returned home to marry. The news following their wedding was expected, his new unit would be deployed in a few months. Off and on through their relationship they had spent much of their time apart, because of school and the Army. "We were pretty much used to it. We knew what to expect." Little surprised her about the entire year he was away. By the time he left they had found housing for her on post. She began to familiarize herself with the Army rules, regulations, and structure. Most importantly, she began to meet other wives who would become close friends over the twelve months Curtis was away.

> "It was easier than I thought. The first couple days were kind of hard; I couldn't sleep. Afterwards, I was feeling a lot better. I started hanging out with friends a whole lot. Then we got the chance to get on the computer and we'd talk all the time. And I was going home all the time, it went by pretty fast."

It wasn't just one thing that helped her, Nicole advocated for herself, and surrounded herself with support. Whether it was other wives or her family, she was always with other people distracting her and talking to her. "It was pretty good, because friends were going through the same thing." She developed a strong bond with a few wives in Curtis' company, but since their return from Iraq they have all moved on to other bases. She feels as though people are leaving all the time. However, Nicole does not feel as though she is confined to their Army post. Traveling to see her family is her primary coping mechanism and has become part of her routine.

> "It's kind of hard to be depressed around my family, because they're crazy. You can't be depressed at my house, you cannot! There is always somebody running into the room, messing with you, sitting on your bed, asking you what you're doing, 'Do you want to play with me?' You just can't, there is just too much going on."

Nicole has made the trip to her home in North Carolina on many occasions. During the deployment, she found it a refuge from the Army life, surrounded by smiling faces and laughter. Traveling broke up the time away from Curtis and kept her busy. While in Iraq, Curtis was an avid Internet user and also did his part keeping her busy from thousands of miles away. The time difference meant that on most occasions she would find herself talking online to her husband in the early morning hours. "He'd page my cell phone, and I'd leave from my bedroom, come in here (the living room), and we'd talk for hours." It made her time alone go by quickly.

Soon, she was back in his arms. After preparing the house for her husband's return, they escaped the Army for a well-deserved trip to Hawaii. The tropical air revived his body from its tiring year in the desert heat. They felt like newlyweds again.

The now wide-eyed little Jay is playing with the gold necklace hanging around his mother's neck. He was born nine months after their relaxing reunion vacation to Hawaii. She sees her tiny bundle as the biggest change between the subsequent deployment and the previous one. When Curtis leaves she will look to family and friends for support, but it will be more challenging, it will be two of them. "It's going to be different. I'm not by myself. I just can't run and get something to eat. I've got to get him dressed, get the car seat, and the stroller, you know. He can be a handful."

Nicole is not in denial of her husband's impending deployment. Neither is she naive to the danger of war. Nicole is simply an Army wife who is confident and content. Instead of stressing over and battling the Army life, she immerses herself, because it appears as though this will be their life for a very long time. Curtis recently re-enlisted. He briefly mentions that he is pretty sure that he would like to stay in for the minimum twenty years to receive retirement benefits. Although he has never spoken those words to her before, it is no surprise. Nicole is supportive of her husband's choice. All that truly matters to her is being a family and having the means to do so.

Connie

Counting Down on the Calendar

"I had anxiety real bad last night.
It felt like I was going to jump out of my skin. I don't know [why].
I know it has to do with him coming home."
- Connie

Connie

She can count the number of days on one hand until her husband will be home. In her brief time as an Army wife she has counted many days. A calendar hangs on her kitchen wall, where the same blue marker has crossed out nearly three hundred and sixty days, each day without her husband. His homecoming has her in preparation mode. While he readies himself at his camp in Iraq, packing bags and tossing unneeded belongings, she cleans the house and gets herself ready. There is a long list of "to do's" beginning with cleaning, cooking, shopping, baking, and more cleaning. She will keep herself busy every waking moment until his arrival home in an effort to make the time pass quickly. Her waking hours are many, she is too anxious and too excited to sleep. But, her eyes are not tired. Instead, her eyes are bright, filled with the excitement of a wife in waiting. A wife who will no longer be alone.

Connie is a modern woman. Much of her life, love and relationships are intertwined with her computer and the Internet. It is no surprise that she needs her computer these days, while her husband, Stephen, is deployed. The Internet has grown into a vital tool in communication, keeping them together through such difficult times. For Connie, the Internet has not only been an asset in keeping their relationship strong, it was also what originally made their relationship possible. Back in high school she was an avid user of Instant Messenger, and began chatting with another high school student, Stephen, on a regular basis. In the entire World Wide Web she managed to find a boy who lived right down the street. They were students at rival high schools in Northern Florida and following the discovery that they were geographically connected; they began dating. At the time, Stephen was already a soldier.

> "It was my senior year. He had already gone to Basic Training; he had gone in the summer (between his junior and senior year). Well, he was in Reserves and at that time he didn't know if he was going Active or not. Then when he graduated and they sent him over to Iraq. As soon as he graduated, he was gone. Well, he thought it was fun."

Although they were neither married nor technically engaged, they were a serious couple. To help her through the deployment, she worked many hours with the two jobs she found after graduating from high school. She tried to make Stephen feel like a part of her life, but his unit was one of the first groups into the combat zone. "They didn't have Internet or phones really set up. They had satellite phones and those are fifteen minutes at a time, so when we did talk it was real short. It was hard. I look back at it now, there is no way I would have made it this time [with the same communication]." When the long year was over, they married, and moved to his next assignment with an Active Duty unit.

The change into Active Duty would come with many adjustments. Stephen had re-classed (changed jobs) to a more dangerous occupation. "He re-classed from Chemical into Combat Engineer, and I was kind of mad at him for that." She was understandably distraught over her husband's new job choice that could potentially put him in harm's way. Regardless of what was happening in his career, she was elated to finally be with Stephen.

Shortly after their arrival to post they were informed that his Active Duty unit was under orders to deploy. She prepared herself for what would be their second yearlong tour of separation. "He left February the second. It was his birthday." Stephen turned twenty-one years old on the plane ride to Iraq. "They told him that he couldn't drink in uniform. It was hard on him (to leave on his birthday). I thought it was kind of funny." This time, things would be very different for Connie. It was a given that the goodbyes would be harsher as his wife, but now she was the sole person the Army brought information to about the deployment. It was a new role. "All the information is going to me and not his parents. I get the information first. I am a different priority; I am number one, instead of number two. I tell them (her in-laws) everything that they need to know. We talk a lot. I tell them important stuff, but I have to be careful." Spouses are warned of the danger of revealing too much information, for fear of it getting out to the general public. The Army gives strict guidelines stating that only immediate family is to be given details, such as dates and the locations of deployments and redeployments.

Today, like every day for the last year, her computer is turned on. Her Instant Messenger is signed in. If her husband happens to be able to get online, it an open door to communication with Connie. Stephen is able to get into the computer lab at his camp in Iraq every few days.

> "It depends on when their missions are. When I do get to talk to him it's usually for about thirty to thirty-five minutes, because he's usually tired, worn out, stinking, and hungry. That's what he does! If he talks

to me in the morning time, he's like, 'Okay I'm going to go eat. I'll talk to you tomorrow.'"

Chatting isn't the only activity they participate in online. By using web cameras they can see one another and send smiles and kisses across the globe. The tiny camera has been irreplaceable to Connie through the year. "Seeing him, knowing he's [okay]. 'What did you do to your head?' That is [something I] actually said to him this year." Stephen had hit his head on the door of his vehicle. Connie has her computer running and logged in at all hours of the day and night. During her few sleeping hours she keeps the volume turned to maximum, so it can wake her up in case he starts to chat during the middle of the night. "It's like a door bell. 'Ding-dong, ding-dong.' And, so I wake up." She says with a screen name like "Ilove*******bear" he really only wants to talk to her. They rarely get interrupted by other people wanting to chat with them online.

Although communication has improved since his last deployment, there has been a dramatic shift in their attitudes towards war and separation. It has been a different experience for them both.

> "He hates being away, I guess it kind of depends on his feeling for the country because he hates [that] country. He hates Iraq. He hates the way it looks, the way it smells, the people within it. He's almost died in that country, because he was in an explosion in May, and he hates it. He wants to go home, the missions suck, and he's done."

The danger has become more real and it is difficult for Connie to repeat some of the stories he tells. It pains her to think that her husband experiences such life-threatening danger everyday and there is nothing she can do to protect him or help him. One incident in May was particularly disturbing and angering for Connie. During one of their online video chats she noticed new markings on his face and neck. She questioned her husband, but he just shrugged as if nothing happened. Connie became more suspicious of an accident after she noticed additional money on their pay invoice from the Army. While on mission, he had been the victim of an improvised explosive device.

> "The Army, they didn't notify me. Stephen told me, he slipped. He wasn't going to tell me, because all he had was cuts and bruises. He wasn't [seriously] hurt. I said, 'Why didn't the Army tell me? [Why didn't they] notify me that my husband was in an explosion in the same day?' But they did financially compensate us. He didn't tell me because

he knew it would scare me. He thought he was looking out for me, which I know he was. I can't be mad at him for it."

The thought of her husband being involved in such a terrible attack, which ultimately killed some of his fellow soldiers, made her sick to her stomach. She was infuriated at the Army for not coming out and telling her about his injuries and involvement in an accident. They later explained to her that he was not severely injured, and could walk away from the scene, so they were not required to inform his next of kin of the attack. She was terrified. With the attack behind them, she knew how important it was for her to be there for Stephen. All she could do was listen.

> "It shook him. Coming close to, you know, [death]. He didn't admit it all the time [that he might be scared]. But, you know, when a soldier cries, it's a big deal when a soldier cries. I think his relationship with Jesus came through on that, because he realized that it is the only reason he is alive. I think he felt a lot of guilt because he felt he had been neglecting his faith."

Looking towards God and faith has been one of the most vital aspects in her ability to survive her husband's daily battle with mortality. "If I did not have prayer, I don't think I'd make it. That's just one of those things you have to do." Connie grew up attending church regularly and now, as a married woman, faith plays a part in her daily routine.

> "Stephen and I have a set of books, it's called "Power of a Praying Wife." He actually started it when he went the first time. He got "Power of a Praying Husband" so we pretty much live out of these books. It teaches you how to pray for your husband, and it teaches him how to pray for his wife, and I do the prayer workbook journal for it. I do that every night."

Routine is important for Connie. The nighttime can be particularly difficult. The house is empty. As she sits on their couch or in their bed, alone, thoughts begin to boil in her head. Sleep has been difficult to achieve throughout the deployment. Connie has been suffering from both sleep and anxiety problems during his time in the Army. "On and off, it's been a problem, so much so that they prescribed me Ambien. I've always been a worrier. I lay down and my mind just won't shut off." Her prescription has helped, primarily because it allows her to have a good night's sleep, without drowsiness. She takes a separate medication for her anxiety, but even when taking it regularly she finds herself suffering at times.

> "I had anxiety real bad last night. That's when I decided to take an Ambien. It felt like I was going to jump out of my skin. I don't know [why]. I know it has to do with him coming home, but a lot of the time when I have anxiety it's just a compilation of everything. I can't pinpoint it."

Connie is not alone in her struggles; Stephen wrestles with his own depression and anxiety. She expects that he will have to seek professional counseling when he returns, and supports him doing so. Connie also sees that for Stephen, there is a much less formal or scientifically proven method of coping. Her husband medicates himself with video games. "I don't know if it is shooting people or what, but it calms him." His "dream-station" is awaiting his arrival back home. Connie admits with pride what a gamer her husband truly is, and how much noise he'll be making in their Army housing when he returns.

Stephen re-enlisted while he was in Iraq. His new contract would put him at eleven total years in the Army, only nine away from his pension. This is one of many reasons that Connie believes her husband to be a "lifer," a soldier who will always be exactly that, a soldier. Along with extending his contract, he also changed his MOS (Military Occupational Specialty) to EOD (Explosive Ordnance Disposal). It is a highly specialized field in the Army, which will require two years of extensive training. "I am looking right now at possibly two years of stabilization, at least." Those years will provide quality time to concentrate on their family. "He's looking for a 'mini me.'" They have been hoping to start their family for some time now. "I just don't think it was time. I was also seventy pounds heavier. [This time] knowing that he's not going back to Iraq anytime soon [will make it better]. That was our deal with the last year. We tried all year, but we knew he was leaving." Beginning the adventure of starting a family is one of many things she looks forward to upon Stephen's return.

> "I just can't wait, though, for this all to be over. This year has gone by so fast. Some days have gone by slowly. But, I can remember, I was taking the trash out one night, and I was walking in. It was starting to get cold, and I just thought to myself, 'I'm walking by myself. This whole year I've walked by myself, and this whole year he has walked by himself.'

And it was a corny moment, but I was thinking, 'Where is this time going?' It doesn't feel like I've walked by myself for a year."

Soon, Connie will not have to walk alone. She is counting the hours to his arrival home. Her mind slips back into preparation mode. This afternoon she will be busy spending time with her close friend and neighbor making signs to welcome their husbands back. She purchased a few full size sheets and seven cans of various colors of spray paint to make their creations. Two of the signs will be displayed in the airfield hangar during the redeployment ceremony. The other sign will be draped from her patio, for all her neighbors to read.

"BUMP IRAQ, MY BABY'S BACK!"

Painting Welcome Sign

Sheila

I'm an Army Wife, I can Handle Anything!

"We always want to [be strong] because we don't want our husbands to be more worried before they get there. It's the hardest thing. We always have to be the strong one, regardless. We have to put up the front, even though we want to break down inside."
~Sheila

Sheila

"She ran around in a circle in the kitchen. [She] couldn't believe it was him; she was just so excited. She would touch his face like this (fingers pressed into his cheeks); she just couldn't believe that he was here. And then, everyday, she made sure he was coming home. Everyday, she had to go and pick him up for lunch to make sure he was there, because she got out of preschool about the same time they get out for lunchtime. Well, now she's okay and settled, but I know as soon as he leaves again, and goes to Iraq, it's going to be the same thing over again. The older she gets the more she'll recognize things; she'll be four in March. It doesn't matter when they leave, it's going to be very heartbreaking for her."

Sheila's daughter is at preschool this morning. Her daily routine has become more stable in the past months following her father's return from his one-year tour in Korea. It was a learning experience for Sheila and her family; things happened that she never anticipated. Though she kept herself busy working to help her cope, her daughter suffered through much of his tour. She was only two when her father, Monty, left. "She didn't take it very well. She started going through separation anxiety. That was tough, so I didn't work an awful lot, but I worked some of the time. She was really going through an awful time." Sheila is a mother and a grandmother, though she has no gray hair to prove it. Her children face their father's absence each in their own way. Her daughter's method is the most heartbreaking.

"She had emotional distress. She was crying, asking for Daddy. Then she got mad [and] didn't want to talk to Daddy. When he came home for Christmas, for 'R and R,' that was the worst thing. It made it worse because he had to go again. She really was emotionally attached to his leg, the whole time. He could not leave her sight for a second. It was sad to see, and I knew it was going to be really, really hard. I'd tell her, 'Daddy's at work, far away, and he can't come home right now. Daddy loves you.' You keep telling them that, but they don't understand, and that's the hardest. When you have to deal with seeing a child going through separation like that, emotionally, it just hurts. But, you know, you have to go on because you have other kids."

Every moment of her eight years of marriage to her husband have been spent in the Army. It has shaped and molded their family into who they are. Monty was in the military before they met, serving three years in the North Carolina National Guard. Most of his time has been in Active Duty, traveling the country and the world, bringing help during natural disasters.

When the couple met through a mutual friend they immediately knew it would be a serious romance. "I met him in February of ninety-eight. We married in March. We didn't realize it at the time, but we went to the Justice of the Peace and got married on his grandparents' anniversary." To help further his career and provide for his new family, he joined the Army full time. It was a decision she has grown more grateful for as the years have gone by. "Job security is not good in North Carolina. You could be in a job for twenty [years], and they could fire you for no reason. What type of security is that? [In] the Army, you're on contract, so it's a safer place to be." Their transition into Active Duty would take them "across the pond." Sheila was excited for the opportunity to travel and see a different part of the world.

Everything about Germany was new. "It's a very different atmosphere, not as high paced." During the three years abroad at their first duty station, Monty spent many months away for training. She calculates that she saw him a total of twelve months of that time. "If anything happens, the men are always gone. [He] was out in the field when he found out I was pregnant." Their family enjoyed their time in Germany to the extent that they requested to stay after his re-enlistment. The Army has strict standards on the length families can stay abroad, and they were sent to their first duty station in the states.

Sheila acknowledges that she has had to adjust to the difficulty of being so far from her parents and their extended family. She bonds with those around her who feel the same way. "I think in the military you are your family, everyone around you becomes your family. As far as our family, they understand it, but it's hard for them." The longer they are in the Army, the more important their Army "family" becomes. Their families, on both sides, have trouble understanding the demands and challenges they face as an Army family.

"We haven't seen our family for three years, until his parents got here last week. They came for a week. That was the first time his dad was ever on a plane. They [had] never come out to see anyone, but we told them there's just no way [we could go to North Carolina]. You want to see your son? Just for the fact that he's going to Iraq, then you're going have to come."

Finding the time and money to see family far from their duty station isn't the only struggle she experiences. She explains that war can be difficult. "His mom is probably taking it the worst." The news of Monty's deployment to Iraq was heartbreaking for their entire family. She sees her in-laws being torn apart. "My husband is an only child, that makes it a little worse for them. My family is not taking it very well either, because they love my husband to death. It's not easy for them."

Monty's unit is scheduled to leave in a number of weeks. Sheila anticipates that it will be a time filled with emotions almost too difficult to bear. She is someone who others look towards for support, as a Point of Contact for her husband's platoon. She will be flooded with calls and e-mails over the next few weeks as the deployment date becomes more final. This goodbye will be much different than anything she has had to do before. She counts herself lucky. While away on tour in Korea she knew he was safe, this is his first time saying goodbye, to step foot into combat.

"We always want to [be strong] because we don't want our husbands to be more worried before they get there. It's the hardest thing. We always have to be the strong one, regardless. We have to put up the front, even though we want to break down inside."

Sheila has learned many ways to cope with separation, but she knows it will be different when she sees him off to war. She has tried to learn from those around her. "Almost all my friends, their husbands are [on their] second tours being there (Iraq). They get off the plane and they're gone [again]." These close friends of hers, wives of soldiers, who are now her second family will help her through the many challenging times ahead. Sheila fears for herself and her ability to handle the deployment. She fears for her children and how they will grow in his absence. She also fears for his safety.

"I know going over there, it would have been much better for him to have gone in the beginning, than it is now. I'm dreading that. I know that if I was going to go to war, I would follow right behind him, because I know he's strong. And because I know he knows what he's doing. After all the years we've been in, he's been through Kosovo and Ecuador and all these other places. I would follow him probably through anything. He knows what he's doing, but that doesn't mean it still can't happen to him. It's like with any of them. I feel for all of the families."

It will be an emotional time. While she takes care of things at home, and takes care of those in her family, she hopes that the community she is in looks at her challenges with compassion. "I think that there should be more understanding," she says, in regards to people in the civilian world. "I think they should be more patient; and know that we may be military, but we're not rich."

"Understand that we are more emotional, and high strung. We get angry easier, because we deal with so much. Taking care of the kids, taking care of the house, it's like being a single parent all the time because they're gone. So, we kind of live in the same situation of those who are single parents. They seem to think that we have everything. We have military housing, but we go through a lot of stuff, living here."

The military experience is not new for Sheila. Her family line has served in various branches throughout the years. She believes that her background helps her to maintain a positive attitude where those around her cannot. "I think for some people, coming into the Army is harder for them." The ever-changing world of the Army will not shake her resolve. She has eight years behind her and many more ahead. Her husband enjoys his job, he feels fulfilled, and she anticipates that he will want to stay in as long as it is beneficial for his career and their family. Sheila envisions her husband finishing his career with nearly thirty years of service behind him. With all the past experiences and even with what lies ahead, she is a positive mother and Army wife. "I wouldn't change any of it."

Menda

Menda's Couch Covered in Children

Menda

*I was told Menda had a full house. She lives with her family in the enlisted hous-
ing, in a split-level, four-bedroom, townhouse-style building, just like thousands of
other Army families. This afternoon Menda is baby-sitting her friend's two preschoolers
while their mother runs errands. All of her own school-aged children are expected home
in the next hour. One by one, they will greet her, each vying for their mother's attention, telling stories about what happened today in school. The eldest arrives and cozies
up to her mother on the couch. The middle-schoolers arrive, followed by the grade-
schoolers. Soon, all seven of Menda's children are home from school. She prepared me
for the chaos, warning of the volume of children that will fill the house. Menda's soft
tone does not waiver. As the volume increases and the chaos overcomes the house, she
remains the calm. The hurricane of children rushes around her, but she is the peaceful
eye of the storm. By the time her youngest arrives, including the two borrowed children
and my own daughter, ten children whirl about the two of us.*

Menda's home is decorated to celebrate the holiday season. Her Army quarters
don't have a fireplace to hang their stockings. Instead, their nine red velvet stockings line the stairwell. Nine stockings, one for her, one for her husband, Monty,
and the other seven for their children. Menda always wanted to have a big family
and a house filled with children. The holidays are a time for joy in their family.
The main reason is that Monty is home. His unit had plans to be in Iraq over
Christmas, but at the last minute the deployment was delayed, allowing families time together over the holidays. Christmas also happens to be when she and
Monty first met at a family Christmas barbecue.

Growing up in their home country of Guam, Monty was the type of boy to
dream big, and planned out his Army career by the age of twelve. He has been in
the Army, through the Reserves and Active Duty, for twenty-two years. Menda
knew what a truly committed soldier he was at their wedding. He wore his Class
A (formal) Uniform as a symbol of their marriage into the military. "I felt like I
wasn't just marrying him, I was marrying the military, becoming a military wife."

Menda says Monty is her "soul partner." They have been married for fifteen years. "I just can't see my life without him."

During their courtship, they spent many months apart due to his career, so Menda expected the challenges. After they started their family, her reasons for staying positive about Army life grew with each new baby. "[Wives] have to stay positive for their kids. I think that is how a lot of women think it through." For Menda, that means being optimistic and having enough strength for each of her seven children when their father is away. But even the strong have moments when they crumble. "My daughter would write to her father when he was in Iraq, and tell him to come home because, 'I hear Mommy crying at night.'" Nighttime is difficult when Monty is away.

> "Inside, I break, but I can't break outside, because of my seven kids. So, I break at nighttime, you know. I hardly sleep when he's gone because I become mother and father. It's very much a hard time because he's not there. I have this big old pillow, I put his t-shirt over it, and I just hug "him." I remember one time spraying his cologne and spraying too much and that it gave me a headache. I just busted into tears because I was like, 'No! I can't even hug the pillow.' I was cussing. 'How could I be so dumb?' I had to wash his shirt. His smell is gone."

Each of Menda's children found their own way to cope with their father's absence. With crayon in hand, her youngest daughter would find pictures of her father and draw an "X" over his face whenever she was angry at him. One of her sons wanted to fill his father's shoes, telling Menda that he was the man of the house while his father was away. "I have to protect you," he told her one evening. She replied, "Son, I'm here to protect you. I'm the adult. You're the child." Being a mother is already challenging enough, but during Monty's deployments and separation from the family, she has twice the parenting work to fulfill. "It's been a struggle because of the fact that there is no family really around [to help] me with the kids and give me that extra break. Because when my husband leaves, my kids become magnets. They don't let me out of their sight, unless they are going to school." The stress gets to her; stress which stems from the children missing their father, and her missing Monty.

Menda found herself falling into a depression while Monty was away. It took another Army family to truly understand and help Menda. A close friend's husband, who is also a soldier, was able to break down her wall, and get her out of the darkness. Friends in the Army have become a vital support system to help her manage. She has made friendships with other wives that she hopes will continue for the rest of her life. They have grown so close because of what they share, a bond unique to those in the military, and the understanding, which comes from being a soldier's wife. That bond also brings hardship, and Menda feels as though a piece of her leaves each time a close friend moves to another post.

Friends have become a second family for Menda. They understand where others do not. Menda is close to her family, but feels they lack compassion and understanding for her life as a soldier's wife. "So, as far as comfort for when he is gone, I only have neighbors and other people who are going through the same thing." Menda longs for her family to reach out and help her in her times of need. Family is extremely important to her, but recently they have been more of a hindrance than help. In order to help, she says that they should try to listen more, and talk less.

> "One of the remarks that they like to say to me is that, 'Well, you knew that's what you were getting into when he joined the Army and you married him. You know that's their life. He's a soldier, you have to tough it out.' They don't even want to listen."

What she would like from her family are more open ears and open hearts, to help her and hear her. In their defense, she says they claim she is the strong one in the family. To her, it doesn't matter if she is the strongest or the weakest she needs their support. She says that, "People need to know," that Army wives want help, they want phone calls from family and friends, and it is vital for their survival. If others were to begin to reach out to military families and wives, Menda believes that they would learn more about the lifestyle and clear up many of the misconceptions. "They think [we're] in the military to have the money rolling in and [we're] living the good life. They actually don't know. We live paycheck to paycheck. I don't complain about it. I'm not a complainer, because I didn't marry my husband for money, anyways. We do what we can do without, it's not going to change our relationship." There are also other misconceptions, in her opinion. She sees others who believe Army wives have, "No reason for us to complain about being apart, when they don't understand." She notes how different her husband's job is compared to an average eight-to-five job. Most families get face-to-face contact with each other every evening when they return home. In her world finding out how Monty's day went can sometimes consist of waiting for the Internet to come back online at Monty's camp after an attack.

Deployments and separation can be strenuous, demanding months. Menda looks to her faith, Buddhism, as a way to balance herself. In her living room they have their family shrine. Menda chants daily for her husband's safety when he is away. His photograph rests on the step of the shrine, surrounded by flowers. The children also chant. "I always tell them to, 'Just pray for your dad.'" Prayer is the only tangible thing that they can do for their father's safety when he is at war. Menda's faith gives her a unique perspective on war. It allows her to see the positives when the negatives blind most.

> "I'm proud of my husband. I'm proud of what he stands for. I'm proud of his accomplishments. I'm very proud to be in the military. I'm very proud. I think it's a great thing that my husband does, what all the soldiers do. I look at the bigger picture. My husband used to tell me I was crazy. He used to get mad, because when [he] told me he was going to Iraq I said, 'You get to put your feet in the muddiest and ugliest swamp of all and you get to be a lotus flower and blossom.' He said, 'What the hell are you saying to me?' I said, 'I am so proud of you.' He looked at me, 'You think I'm taking my boots off and sticking my feet in something nasty!' I said, 'No, you get to be a lotus flower where there is ugliness in this world, to be there to make a difference, and help make a difference.' He said, 'I don't see it Menda. This is war.'"

Menda experiences her husband's love for the Army everyday. He recently decided to reenlist during a time when retention is low, and bonuses are high, but for Monty it's not about the money. "He loves the military." His work is a twenty-four hour job, and Menda believes that, "They are not appreciated enough, because when it's time for war, they have to go. Monty may not want to leave, but that is his job." He has spent one tour in Iraq, and is scheduled to leave for a second tour in the summer of 2006. Menda will once again provide guidance and love for her seven children at home, while he will write and call home in order to parent from afar.

> "My favorite thing when he was in Iraq [is when] I would look out and look at the stars and I would hope that he would be looking at that exact star."

Menda and Her Eldest Daughter

Part 5

Homecoming

Love the Welcome Home

Homecoming

Signs Hanging

Wives Waiting to Hang Signs

"Home Is Where The Heart Is"

Homecoming

Standing behind a young woman with glistening red hair, I wait. She is gripping her friend's side, bouncing up and down, giddy in anticipation. She tells her girl-friend how she couldn't sleep at all last night. She looks very young, but is almost certainly waiting for her husband. They stand behind a row of family members forming a tunnel of signs and people for soldiers to walk through. An announcer speaks over the intercom, welcoming friends and family to the redeployment ceremony. The crowd cheers. Only a few minutes left.

There are rows and rows of friends, wives, husbands, and children. The crowd is gathered in Hangar 817 on a Thursday afternoon. Many of these family members were only given a few hours notice of the exact time of the ceremony for security purposes. The walls of the hangar, which normally holds parts to helicopters and Humvees, is lined with homemade signs and posters, each one welcoming home a hero. The centerpiece is an American flag larger than life. More than a story high, it is a statement hard to ignore, and easy to celebrate. Scattered among the crowd are bouquets of balloons, mostly in red, white, and blue. Children and spouses hold up posters, letting their soldiers know where they are in the stands, so they can be sure to make eye contact and to meet up with one another, as soon as possible. Wives are dressed up, with beautiful makeup and elegant hairdos. Other family members wear t-shirts and hats with their soldier's name and rank, celebrating their pride. The excitement is overwhelming to the senses. My heart quickens with every passing moment.

Then, they hear the words they have been waiting twelve months for, "Here they come." Everyone is on their feet. Cheers fill the hangar. The flag of streamers carrying the unit's battles, citations, and honors comes through the door, followed by the unit's commander. The blinding sunlight coming through the hangar door flickers as, one by one, soldiers step through the door. Family members call out and cheer once they get a glimpse of their soldier. Cameras and video recorders capture the unforgettable moments. A few wives are jumping up and down besides me, waving their arms in the air over the crowd, as they see their husbands walk by. The red headed girl grips her friend, she can't stop shaking, and her thin pale legs knock together in excitement. Here love is vibrant and refreshing. In all the excitement and joy, there is so much love.

When all the soldiers stand together in formation, the ceremony begins. The Chaplain leads the entire hangar in a prayer, thanking God for the safe arrival and return of so many soldiers. Next, the National Anthem is played; much of the audience sings and cheers along with each verse. The crowd roars as the commander begins his speech to the company. With some "Welcome home's" and a few "Hooah's," he greets his soldiers and the audience. He speaks about the mission they just accomplished and how much of a difference they have been able to make in Iraq. In the same way a father is proud of his children, he speaks with pride about how they served their country and the world. His voice turns solemn as he asks the crowd to join him in a moment of silence, to remember those who did not return. All heads bow. The commander reads the name of the soldiers and recognizes their families present in the audience.

The soldiers are in formation in front of the gigantic flag, surrounded by their joyous families. They are wearing their DCU's and matching boonie or field caps. One soldier in the front stands with crutches. Some are able to find their loved ones in the stands. They give a nod, wink, or smile, for that special someone who has waited so long to see them again. The anticipation of holding their spouse in their arms is in their eyes. Their hearts pace in excitement as their legs are glued to the floor in formation. The commander gives one last order to his soldiers. "Go find your family. Fall out!"

The perfect formation disperses as the crowds in the stands and on the floor go to meet them. Some run, some jump, some squeal, some kneel, some cry, some smile, some scream, some pray, and they all hug. Wives and husbands clench each other, holding one another so tightly that it almost hurts to let go. Babies are held by their fathers for the first time, tiny infants surrounded by camouflage. Families pose for pictures. Children are held high in the air, resting on Daddy's shoulders. Moms and Dads hold their soldiers, thankful they are home safe, worry stripped away. Everyone is filled with love, covering each other with hugs and kisses. It is a beautiful moment, just as I always imagined it would be.

Couple's Embrace

Part 6

Afterword

About the Author and Epilogue

My Story

Open Hands

My Story

I should have known. For months it was a toss up between Special Forces and the CIA. It would have been obvious to anyone. The truth is that most girls who get engaged to someone in college believe that there is a plan. If a man goes to a university they should have a career in mind, and you two will live happily every after. That career, of course, has usually nothing to do with the military, especially for me when I met an Art, Spanish, and International Relations triple major. I guess it never occurred to me that he was so serious about the military life. I thought it was a phase. I thought he was just feeling his own mortality in the plight of graduating during one of the worst years of job cuts in decades. I should have known because at the age of seventeen he came to his parents with the paperwork to join the Marines. They lived only a few miles south of Coronado in San Diego, California, where the Navy Seals train. Frightened at the prospect, his parents told him to apply to colleges instead.

Steve and I met during a language immersion trip to Buenos Aires, Argentina. He was there to complete his major requirements for Spanish, and I was there to complete my foreign language credits, and to "find myself" in a foreign land. For the first two weeks, he only spoke to me in Spanish. I understood and would reply in English, but soon enough he realized, if our friendship were to grow, he would have to slip in some English now and again. It may sound terribly romantic, but our first kiss was in Brazil. A little over two years later, we had our first kiss as husband and wife. The time in between was when things brought us to the Army.

We got engaged during our senior year at our California beach college. It was a year filled with rigorously packed academic schedules and school activities. I had the all-important internship at the most prestigious agency I could find, a path that, at the time, seemed very clear. He, on the other hand, began to search for a career direction. Unlike in years past when graduating seniors found employers knocking on their doors before December with grand offers, our graduating class was struggling. We had hit the online bust year. Employment was at a stand still. People wanted interns, but who could really afford to live in Southern California without an income? The ideals were gone. When I had applied to this university I had everything planned out, and now the plan was flawed. The jobs were not there. After working so hard, we had nothing to show for it. Steve, with his three degrees in four years, and me, with my one degree in three years, and nothing.

Steve began looking into areas where his education could prove valuable, like the military and the CIA. With his extensive cultural background he seemed a perfect fit. He took me to a Special Forces recruiter in Los Angeles. I was far from thrilled. At lunch, afterwards, I told him that if he wanted to have children and say goodbye to them "X" number of times, then I would think about it. The War on Terror was everywhere, I was scared thinking what the future might bring to children left behind. Essentially my answer was, 'not with me, you won't.'

Graduation came and went. Neither of us had careers. We moved into my parents' house. Well, I did. My father made him a great extra bedroom in the garage and, believe it or not, he liked it. Student loan notices began to arrive. With the retail jobs we were currently holding there would be no way to break even. Frustrated, confused, angered, Steve left me in Seattle to try to find a job back with his parents and instead he found his way to an Army recruiter. Burdened by daily news of wounded and dying soldiers, Steve felt a need to assist in some way. It was then that he decided he could contribute most by saving lives. He tested and found the Combat Medic was his best option. The training would be irreplaceable, and they offered to pay off any of his federal student loans from college. He signed up and swore into the Army. A few months later, and a couple moves, and I was in Texas, the home of the Combat Medic training center.

We married on a Sunday evening in August in Bellevue, Washington, with many friends and family. We had just three weeks to be newlyweds before he was shipped off to Basic Training. Looking back, I know how naive I was at the time. I knew it was going to be a hard few months of being away, but I truly had no clue. I was clueless and I was pregnant when he left for basic. We didn't actually find out I was pregnant until a month later. It was a surprise honeymoon baby.

I was working full time with a job in retail, and living alone for the first time in my life, in a new city far from friends and family. I was sad and alone. When I received Steve's first letter I could barely stand to read it, I was just too emotional. When I finally had his address to write him back, my words were full of sadness, I was depressed. Steve knew that something was terribly wrong. He managed to get a two-minute phone call; a couple weeks prematurely in boot camp standards, to phone me and see how serious things were at home.

My phone rang while I was picking up work supplies. An unknown number. "Janelle?" a hoarse voice says on the other line.

"Steve, is that you?"

"Babe, it's me. I just got your letter." I hear the immense worry in his voice. "Is everything okay? You sound awful in the letter. I only have a couple minutes, but you had me so worried." He now has tears in his eyes.

"Oh, honey, things are okay." I feel remorseful that I had worried him so much. By this day I had already gone to the doctors to confirm my pregnancy. I was eight weeks pregnant, and he was about to find out he was going to be a father. I was smiling. With tears in my eyes, I rushed out of the store to be in a more private place to reveal the news. "Hold on just a second, I'm in the store by our house, I'm going to get out. Yeah, everything is okay. I'm okay, but there is something that I have to tell you."

"Well, what is it? I don't have much time."

"We're going to have a baby."

"What? Really? Well, that was unexpected, I mean-"

"Yeah, I know, but I went to the doctor and everything to make sure."

"Are you okay then? You, and the baby okay?"

"Yes, we are. We're okay." Our call quickly ended.

Standing in the parking lot outside, I smiled and wept in shock that I had just spoken to my husband.

All mothers know the hormones that arrive with pregnancy; mine were agitated by the fact that I was alone. I would come home from a long day at work and collapse on the floor in tears. Our dog would sniff and lick my tears away. Reluctantly, I would get enough energy to take her on a walk. Things continued like that for months. I tried as hard as I could to stay positive, knowing that my mental state could impact the baby growing inside me, but I was depressed. I longed for him daily, and nighttime was the hardest time of the day. I could manage work, bills, groceries, the simple things, but I felt so much more alone at night. Steve had always helped me to go to sleep. Alone, in our king size bed, the sheets felt cold and lonely, even in the Texas heat. I slept only from the exhaustion of working on my feet and being pregnant.

Those months were a trying time for me in so many ways. Steve would write me letters, sometimes he would have to wake up at 3 AM just to find the time to do so, but somehow reading them was too difficult for me. It was as if they brought the reality of his inexistence in my life to the forefront. I can't quite explain it, but the letters would accumulate next to my bed, and if I got up enough courage, I would read them, and try to smile through the tears. I kept all the letters, and I have to confess that some of them are still sealed. Denial, I guess. Steve was upset, for obvious reasons, when he found those letters, by my bed, unopened and unread. I greatly regret not reading them when they arrived, and I am still troubled by the reasons they remained untouched.

Instead of counting down the days until his return like a normal human being, other things began to grow in meaning, and took the place of the average calendar. Like the date on the milk carton or orange juice I would buy every week. One day, I looked and realized that by the time this juice went bad, he would be home. Well, actually, he would be at AIT (Advanced Individual Training), but we would finally see each other for the first time in months, knowing that I was carrying our child.

During AIT he was a little over an hour away from our apartment. I would drive to see him when he was allowed. My belly grew bigger with each visit. His training continued for months and at eight months pregnant he graduated, and we were moved. I had to leave my salary job and new friends and move somewhere I had never been before.

Everything was so different. We were officially an Army family. We were blessed to receive housing on post right away. I nested and, at eight and a half months, painted three rooms in our apartment, so it would feel more like home. The baby's room had green hills and a blue sky with white clouds. On May 5th, our baby was born, healthy and beautiful. I called my mother to surprise her that it was a girl, and that we named the baby after her.

With no family around, we were new parents with a crash course in baby everything. Steve was fortunate to have a platoon sergeant that let him have time off to spend with the baby and me. Eventually, my parents came to see their first grandchild, and so did his mother and father. Things were happy and stable for the moment. We adjusted to Army life. Signing up for WIC checks was one of those adjustments. There isn't much money in the Army, at least for us. I made much more with my retail salary than Steve did in the Army. We earn so little month-to-month that we qualify for food checks, which are very helpful. This was certainly a life adjustment coming from a family where I was raised in the upper middle class. I don't complain about our finances, but we don't break even every month, we owe too much. Car payments, insurance, school loans, phone, Internet, it adds up to more than what we make. We have to dip into our savings. I keep a positive attitude because of the medical coverage we get and nothing can replace full coverage when you have a new baby.

I had the opportunity to work and make about half what I was making on salary, but I chose to put my family first. Steve was scheduled to deploy and something irked me inside every time he had to come home to an empty house while I was at work. For the little I would earn, it wasn't worth being away from him, or from our daughter. I would rather be there everyday he comes home for lunch, to make him tuna melts and orange slices. I wanted to be there because for one entire year I wouldn't be able to do that for him. The other thought in the back of my mind was that, if anything ever happened to him in war, I wouldn't want to have any regrets. I would want to be able to look back and know that I was there for him, and I spent all the time with him that I could.

Originally, we had come to our new post with the fear that Steve would have to deploy to Iraq. His unit was first given specific orders, which would have deployed him about the time that our daughter was six months old. The Army is a constantly evolving and adjusting organism. His orders changed. It was frustrating for a time, not knowing if your husband will be leaving in a couple weeks or not. We had many goodbyes with family. I think he said goodbye to his parents, thinking he wouldn't see them for over a year, at least, a couple times. It was irritating, but how unhappy could I really be that my daughter's daddy could be there for her first word? her first step? her first Birthday?

Steve's aspirations in the Army are as high as the moon some days and deep into the sea the next. He loves it, I know it, but he doesn't like having to be away from us. It's hard to explain to people that your husband wants to go to war, but he does. He wants the experience. That is what he is trained to do. He feels as though he can't really know how long he wants to be in the Army until he has that experience behind him. I want what is best for him. I fear the danger of war, but I know he will not feel complete doing time in the Army until he sets foot on foreign soil. I am afraid, but I have to have a peace about it, because if I don't, I won't survive if he doesn't return. We have a peace that, whether together or apart, we are a family, always. I don't know exactly how or why I feel this way. Maybe, it's because my husband has been a Christian all his life. I can't put into words what type of peace that brings. Death, injury, or deployment, we are a family. I will always stand by my soldier and I will always stand by my husband.

Daddy's Kiss Bye-Bye
Deployment Day

Epilogue

The Making of this Book

While writing this book I was constantly amazed. There were so many reasons to be amazed by these women, not just by their words, but also by their actions. Cliché or not, the actions of these Army wives truly speak louder than their words. Through their oral histories they try to convey the overwhelming emotional roller coaster that is their life in the Army. *Grace* might be a good word to describe their actions in many cases. I may be generalizing, but there were many graceful moments that they described in their lives, whether they agree or not. Handed awesome difficulties they made it through. You cannot help but be amazed and even surprised by their words.

Each interview was filled with hours of words to tell the story of their life in the Army. Listening opened my ears, but it also opened my eyes. Each time I observed a home decorated with important family mementos and Army paraphernalia. Each house is still engraved in my mind. It was an experience to see into the eyes of a wife who has seen so much. Eyes always have that ability to add to the words spoken; the photographs serve as an emotional paintbrush, coloring the story in the rainbow of emotion. Some of these women had eyes of joy and pride. Others had eyes full of anger and grief. Most touching were the eyes welling with tears and sadness. It was in those moments that time stood still. That is when publishing this book became more of a mission than an aspiration.

The photographs give brief glimpses into the world of an Army wife. I attempted to use the camera as a way to give the ultimate personal touch to their story. Often, homemade dolls, signs, and other objects represented their life and I felt others deserved to see these. Most civilians may have never otherwise had the opportunity to see these objects of affection and meaning. They would go on living their lives, knowing very little about the Army world. I hope these photographs open their eyes to this other world, this other life.

My amazement grew over the months and so did my passion for this project. The more I heard, the more I wanted others to hear. Any time I mentioned the book's premise to a civilian they immediately became curious and inquisitive. I knew it would be something different, something no one had ever done before.

These thoughts were etched into my mind and helped me to stay focused, even when my own world was being turned upside down.

The generosity of these wives was overwhelming. I traveled with my infant daughter while conducting interviews and she was showered with gifts from baby food to baby toys and baby clothes. I was offered cooking lessons, furniture, baby-sitting, and much more. And it was I who had asked so much of these women. I had entered into their lives and asked them to reveal so much of themselves. It was a shock to see them being so kind and giving. I am extremely grateful and I want them to know how thoughtful their kindness was. It did not go unnoticed or unappreciated. Thank you.

Most importantly, I am grateful for this opportunity. After each interview and the glimpse into the life of a new individual, I become more inspired. I reflected on how remarkable each woman's words were. I felt the need to scream to the world, 'Listen! Listen to this woman and what she has been through. It will amaze you. You need to know.' This book is that scream, only louder.

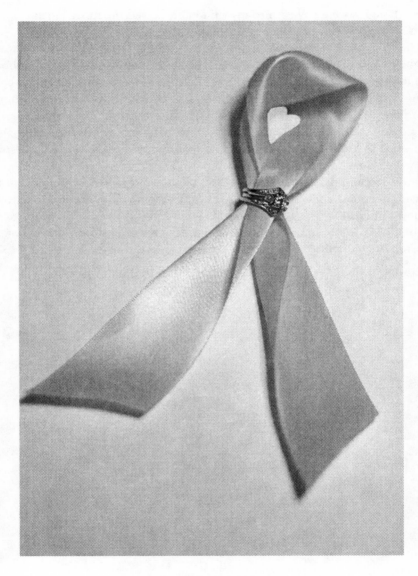

Yellow Ribbon with Ring

Appendix

Glossary of Terms

GLOSSARY
Note: Please be aware that these are not comprehensive definitions of the following terms. These are merely tools to aid the reader in gaining a better understanding of what the persons interviewed are saying.

AAFES: Army and Air Force Exchange Service. A military-operated retail establishment, located on bases across the globe. AAFES sells a variety of goods to meet the needs of the Armed Services and their families.

Ambien: A drug available by prescription indicated for the short-term treatment of insomnia.

ACS: Army Community Service. Provides a variety of services, including food, clothing, and furniture, for soldiers and their families especially during times of need.

Active Duty: Term commonly used to refer to soldiers who work full-time for the United States Army.

ACU: Army Combat Uniform. A new uniform for the Army that is made of a digitized pattern of green and gray designed to be used in any environment.

Air Assault: An additional skill taught to soldiers in order to participate in operations that involve rappelling from rotary-wing aircraft (helicopters).

Airborne: An additional skill taught to soldiers in order to participate in operations that involve jumping from airplanes with parachutes.

AIT: Advanced Individual Training. The school a soldier attends to receive specific training in his field before going to his first duty assignment.

ANCOC: Advanced Non-Commissioned Officers Course. An MOS-specific course for senior Non-Commissioned Officers necessary to be promoted to Master Sergeant or First Sergeant.

Armor: A Combat Arms branch of the Army implementing armored equipment and vehicles in support of combat operations. Currently, the most well known armored vehicle is the M1A1 Abrams tank. This branch is limited to males only.

Army base (Post): A base or group of installations for which a local commander is responsible, consisting of facilities necessary for support of Army activities including security, internal lines of communications, utilities, plants and systems, and real property for which the Army has operating responsibility.

Basic Training: Also known as "boot camp." A rigorous ten-week course designed to train and indoctrinate trainees in order to become soldiers.

BDU: Battle Dress Uniform. The older green, brown, and black uniform that is being phased out and replaced by the new ACU. It can still be seen worn by soldiers and units who do not deploy.

Change of Command: The process of changing commanders of a unit accompanied by a ceremony for Company sized elements and larger.

Command: The authority that a commander in the Armed Forces lawfully exercises over subordinates by virtue of rank or assignment. Command includes the authority and responsibility for effectively using available resources and for planning the employment of, organizing, directing, coordinating, and controlling military forces for the accomplishment of assigned missions.

Chain of command: The succession of commanding officers from a superior to a subordinate through which command is exercised.

"Chemical": Chemical, biological, radioactive, nuclear, environmental (also known as "CBRNE"). The methods, plans, and procedures involved in establishing and executing defensive measures against attack utilizing any of the above.

CIA: Central Intelligence Agency. The United States' main intelligence gathering organization.

Class A Uniform: A formal uniform that displays personal and unit awards, citations, and skills, worn largely by enlisted soldiers when attending formal functions, to perform certain duties, and when presenting before a board for promotion or other reasons. It is "Army green" in color.

Combat Arms: Those forces whose primary missions are to participate in combat and the destruction of enemy forces and/or installations.

Combat zone: Any area forward of the Army rear area boundary where combat takes place.

Combat Medic: Designated medical personnel who are attached to Combat Arms units.

Commission: A written order giving a person rank and authority as an officer in the armed forces.

Commissary: A retail establishment on Army bases available to soldiers, their dependents, and retirees that provides the necessities for living, especially food, at very low prices.

Company: A unit element that is comprised of anywhere from a hundred to several hundred soldiers.

Department of the Army: The executive part of the Department of the Army at the seat of government and all field headquarters, forces, Reserve Components, installations, activities, and functions under the control or supervision of the Secretary of the Army.

Deployment: An assignment that typically lasts one year involving the relocation of forces and materiel to desired areas of operations in a combat zone. Deployment encompasses all activities from origin or home station through destination.

Deployable: Term used to describe an organization's or a soldier's ability to participate in an actual engagement or in support of wartime operations.

"Dog" tags: A set of metal identification tags on a chain that hang from a soldier's neck. They are considered to be part of a soldier's uniform.

DCU: Desert Camouflage Uniform. A tan uniform that is still in use for soldiers in Iraq, but is gradually being phased out and replaced by the new ACU.

Draft: The conscription of qualified citizens in military service. A draft does not currently exist in the United States.

Dress Blue Uniform: A variant of the Class A uniform that displays personal and unit awards, citations, and skills, worn largely by Officers when attending formal functions and to perform certain duties. It is blue in color with gold trim and lace.

Drill Sergeant: A Non-Commissioned Officer whose main responsibility is the training, disciplining and indoctrination of initial entry trainees.

Duty station: Another term to describe Army bases around the world and in the United States where soldiers are assigned for typically one to three years.

Engineer: Branch of the Army specializing in building structures, developing civil works programs, working with natural resources, and providing combat support.

EOD: Explosive Ordnance Disposal. A high demand occupation specializing in the disarming and disposal of explosives and bombs.

FRG: Family Readiness Group. A support group and information network that is formed by the families of soldiers including spouses and parents of unmarried soldiers.

"Full Battle Rattle": A nickname for the equipment carried by the individual soldier into battle including body armor, ammunition, weapon systems, and supplies.

G.I. Bill: Federal financial aid provided to soldiers should they choose to pursue additional education including certification, technical skills, and/or college.

Hooah: A general term used in the Army with any number of different meanings that may convey enthusiasm or acknowledgment.

Improvised Explosive Device: Also called IED. A device placed or fabricated in an improvised manner incorporating destructive, lethal, noxious, pyrotechnic, or incendiary chemicals and designed to destroy, incapacitate, harass, or distract.

Infantry: The Army's main land combat force. Infantry soldiers specialize in combat on all levels, including hand-to-hand combat, a large number of weapon systems, maneuvering vehicles, and communications. This branch is limited to males only.

JRTC: Joint Readiness Training Center. A massive training exercise that incorporates multiple units in preparation for operations in the combat zone.

"Med board": Officially known as a MEB or Medical Evaluation Board. A process by which soldiers can either be retained or separated from the Army due to health issues.

Military Police: The law enforcement branch of the military. Military police operate in much the same manner as civilian police. However, military police also conduct a large number of combat operations when deployed.

MOS: Military Occupational Specialty. A school with specialized job training that an initial entry trainee attends before they are assigned to their first duty station.

National Guard: A state-funded branch of the Army similar to the Reserves in that they train one weekend a month and two weeks a year with the possibility of being called on to deploy. However, they also provide support and aid during national crisis.

OEF: Operation Enduring Freedom. The majority of this military operation is taking place in Afghanistan.

Officer: Soldiers who often operate on an organizational or administrative tier who also supervise and participate in combat operations. They are the leaders of the Army. Officers have an Associates Degree or higher.

OIF: Operation Iraqi Freedom. The majority of this military operation is taking place in Iraq.

Physical Training: Also known as P.T. Every morning at 6:30 AM soldiers gather together in formations and salute the United States flag. They then conduct strength, endurance, and stamina training for an hour. This is done every day of the work week with the exception of National holidays.

Platoon: An element that ranges from twenty to fifty soldiers divided into smaller groups called squads.

Platoon leader: An Officer that serves as a liaison between the platoon and the company commander.

Platoon sergeant: A senior Non-Commissioned Officer who is in charge of a platoon.

Point of Contact: A person through whom other people receive information.

Power of attorney: A legal document granting a designated person certain powers over finances, property, taxes, etc. by the owner of said belongings for a predetermined amount of time.

PTSD: Post-Traumatic Stress Disorder. A medical illness that is still being researched at this time that is caused by traumatic incidents, often during battle.

Purple Heart: An award given to service members who have received wounds during combat.

PX: Post Exchange. A local, government-operated, retail establishment. See AAFES.

Ranger School: A grueling, physically and mentally demanding, two month long course with a high attrition rate whose graduates earn the distinction of being called Rangers. See Rangers.

Rangers: Rapidly deployable airborne light infantry organized and trained to conduct highly complex joint direct action operations in coordination with or in support of other special operations units of all Services.

"R and R": Rest and Recuperation. A period of approximately two weeks when a soldier is allowed to go home while he is deployed.

Re-deployment: To return personnel, equipment, and materiel to the home and/or demobilization stations for reintegration and/or out-processing after a deployment.

Reserve(s): Members of the Military Services who are not in active service but who are subject to call to Active Duty and who train one weekend a month and two weeks a year.

ROTC: Reserve Officer Training Corps. A program that college students can enroll in, accompanied by military education and training, at the end of which they receive their Commissions and become Officers in one of the military branches.

"Rucksack": A sturdy, framed backpack that soldiers use to carry their equipment and clothing.

Scout: A job similar to that of an Infantryman's. It differs in that they operate in smaller units and specialize in reconnaissance and intelligence gathering.

SEAL: Sea, Air, Land. Elite Navy Special Forces unit that conduct special operations. See also Special Forces.

Sergeant: A Non-Commissioned Officer. This rank is mainly responsible for supervising and training the majority of lower enlisted soldiers including all privates and specialists.

Special Forces: Those Active and Reserve Component forces of the Military Services designated by the Secretary of Defense and specifically organized, trained, and equipped to conduct and support special operations.

STOP-LOSS: A condition that prevents soldiers from leaving the Army or retiring due to an upcoming deployment. It is a presidential authority under Title 10 US Code 12305.

Stabilization: A period of three to six months following a deployment or hardship tour when a soldier cannot deploy again or be assigned to another hardship tour.

UN: United Nations. An organization that is comprised of many of the world's nations in an effort to promote peace, financial stability, and human rights.

VA: Veterans Administration. A massive organization dedicated to aiding veterans through healthcare, victim advocacy, and proposing new legislation and programs.

West Point: The United States military's university, the graduates of which becomes Officers in one of the branches of the armed services.

WIC: Women, Infants, Children. A program designed to aid citizens of the United States who fall beneath the poverty line by providing certain essential foods for the diets of women, infants and children. Most junior enlisted soldiers' families qualify for this program. This program has different names in different states.

Resources

There are a growing number of private citizens and organizations actively helping to support military members and their families. Please always research any organization before making monetary donations.

The following is a list of the author's recommendations for resource links and short descriptions from their websites

Websites to offer help to military families across the country:

The Fisher House: www.fisherhouse.org

"Supporting America's military in their time of need, we provide "a home away from home" that enables family members to be close to a loved one at the most stressful time—during hospitalization for an illness, disease or injury."

The Intrepid Fallen Heroes Fund: www.fallenheroesfund.org/fallenheroes/index.php

"The Intrepid Fallen Heroes Fund is constructing a world-class state-of-the-art advanced training skills facility at Brooke Army Medical Center in San Antonio, Texas. The center will serve military personnel who have been catastrophically disabled in operations in Iraq and Afghanistan. The center will also serve military personnel and veterans severely injured in other operations and in the normal performance of their duties, combat and non-combat related."

America Supports You: www.AmericaSupportsYou.mil

"Thousands of Americans are already showing their support for our military men and women. You can join the team, send messages to the troops, and obtain materials for developing your own support program."

Scholarships for Military Children: www.militaryscholar.org

"Commissaries are an integral part of the quality of life offered to service members and their families. The Scholarships for Military Children Program was created in recognition of the contributions of military families to the readiness of the fighting force and to celebrate the role of the commissary in the military family community. It is the intent of the program that a scholarship funded through contributions be awarded annually for each commissary operated by the Defense Commissary Agency worldwide."

Hero Miles: Donate your air miles to U.S. Military Family Members
http://www.fisherhouse.org/programs/heroMiles.shtml

To help our soldiers please visit:

The USO: www.uso.org

"The USO is a private, nonprofit organization whose mission is to provide morale, welfare and recreation-type services to our men and women in uniform. The original intent of Congress—and enduring style of USO delivery—is to represent the American people by extending a touch of home to the military. The USO currently operates more than 120 centers worldwide, including seven mobile canteens located in the continental United States and overseas."

Resources for Military families and spouses:

Army Family Team Building (AFTB): www.myarmylifetoo.com

"AFTB is a volunteer-led organization with a central tenet: provide training and knowledge to spouses and family members to support the total Army effort. Strong families are the pillar of support behind strong Soldiers. It is AFTB's mission to educate and train all of the Army in knowledge, skills, and behaviors designed to prepare our Army families to move successfully into the future."

Military OneSource: www.militaryonesource.com

"Whether its help with child care, personal finances, emotional support during deployments, relocation information, or resources needed for special circumstances, Military OneSource is there for military personnel and their families … 24/7/365!"

Recourses to learn more about the Army and military family members:

U.S. Army Official Website www.goarmy.com

The Army Times (weekly periodical): www.armytimes.com

Military Spouse Magazine (bi-monthly periodical):
www.militaryspousemagazine.com

Please visit www.janellemock.com
for the most up-to-date list of resources and links
to non-profit organizations.

Are you an Army or military family member who would like to be
involved in one of Janelle Mock's upcoming book projects?
Please visit her website to contact her with your personal stories
www.janellemock.com.

Upcoming titles
from Janelle Mock:

Portraits of
The Toughest Job in the Army
VOLUME II

Portraits of
The Toughest Kids in the Army

&

Portraits of
The Greatest Sacrifice in the Army

Endnotes

1 Donna Miles, "Army Divorce Rates Drop as Marriage Programs Gain Momentum." [Available online]

American Forces Press Service, United States Department of Defense [cited January, 2007]; Available from: http://www.defenselink.mil/news/Jan2006/20060127_4034.html.

2 Department of Defense, "Military Divorce Rates Spurs Action." [Available online]

Website for Military Spouses [cited January, 2007]; Available from: http://www.military.com/spouse/fs/0,fs_marriage_divorce,00.html?ESRC=family.nl.

978-0-595-42615-7
0-595-42615-8

Printed in the United States
112450LV00003B/265-267/A